India 1900–47

Rosemary Rees

Series Editors
Martin Collier
Rosemary Rees

Heinemann

HEINEMANN ADVANCED HISTORY

Heinemann Educational Publishers
Halley Court, Jordan Hill, Oxford OX2 8EJ
Part of Harcourt Education

Heinemann is the registered trademark of
Harcourt Education Limited

© Harcourt Education, 2006

First published 2006

10 09 08 07 06 05
10 9 8 7 6 5 4 3 2 1

British Library Cataloguing in Publication Data is available
from the British Library on request.

13-digit ISBN: 978 0 435327781

Edited by Susan Milligan   Commissioning Editor – Kate Lowe
Proof read by Kathy Peltan   Managing Editor – Simon Brand
Indexed by Eleanor Holme   Production controller – David Poole
Typeset by TechType

Original illustrations © Harcourt Education Limited, 2006
Illustrated by TechType

Printed in Great Britain by Scotprint

Cover photo: © Scala

Picture research by Natalie Gray

Acknowledgements
The author and publisher would like to thank the following for permission to reproduce:

Photographs – 17th century painting of the court of the Emperor Akbar, Chester Beatty library; Mughal Emperor
Farrukhsiyar (1701-1719), Mary Evans; William Palmer with his two Indian wives, daughter and two of his sons,
together with three other women by Francesco Renaldi in 1786, British Library shelf number Foster 597, British
Library, London; A family of 'untouchables' in front of their house, Time & life Pictures/ Getty Images; Calcutta
Golf Club, 1910, popperfoto; Celebrations in a princely state where a new mararajah has succeeded to the throne,
TopFoto / PA; The 1911 Delhi durbar, Hulton Archive / Getty; British soldiers enforcing the 'Crawling Order',
Courtesy of the Council of the National Army Museum; Gandhi spinning thread, Hulton Archive / Getty;
A demonstration against the presence of the Simon Commission, Hulton Archive / Getty; Some of Gandhi's
followers boiling sea water to extract salt, Bettmann/CORBIS; Muhammad Ali Jinnah, popperfoto; Punch cartoon
of January 1931, Mansell Collection / Getty; The Round Table conference held at St James' Palace, London, in
1931, Topham / Dinodia; Gandhi with the Viceroy and Lady Mountbatten, Hulton Archive / Getty; A town in
the Punjab after days of Hindu / Muslim rioting, Bettmann/CORBIS; Jawaharlal Nehru taken in 1947, Hulton
Archive / Getty

Every effort has been made to contact copyright holders of material reproduced in this book. Any omissions will be
rectified in subsequent printings if notice is given to the publishers.

This book is dedicated to my cousin, Elisabeth Bown, with whom I first visited India.

HEINEMANN ADVANCED HISTORY

CONTENTS

HEINEMANN ADVANCED HISTORY

HOW TO USE THIS BOOK

This book is designed and written to meet the content and assessment requirements of Edexcel's AS paper 'India 1900–47'. It is anticipated that it will also be of use to students studying the years to Indian independence for coursework and for the written papers of other Awarding Bodies. Although primarily aimed at AS students, it is hoped that GCSE students, wishing to extend and deepen their understanding of India at this time, will find much to interest them here.

The main section of the book describes and explains the important political developments, together with their social and economic context, in India between 1900 and 1947. It focuses on the ways in which Britain and the Raj tried to adapt to Indian demands for independence; on developments within India resulting in the emergence of the Congress Party and the Muslim League, and their different needs within the context of a general demand for independence; on the growth of the idea of Pakistan and finally on the creation of the separate states of India and Pakistan and the carnage that resulted from Partition. The text of this narrative aims to give the student in-depth information and some basic analysis. The summary questions at the end of each chapter challenge the student to use the information to explain, evaluate and analyse important aspects of the topic covered by that chapter. In this way, students will acquire a clear understanding of the key features of each topic.

The main focus of the Assessment section is on Edexcel's requirements at AS. Here two questions are unpacked and advice given about planning and writing responses.

A detailed modern map of India, showing important places mentioned in this book, follows this section and it is recommended that students familiarise themselves with the basic geography of India before embarking on the main text, as well as using the map as a point of reference as they work through the text.

At the end of the book students will find a glossary and a bibliography. The bibliography suggests the mainstream books that students may wish to consult. It also gives a selection of documentary readings together with suggestions about appropriate contemporary accounts and relevant fiction. Students are strongly advised to broaden their understanding of the period by reading as widely as possible.

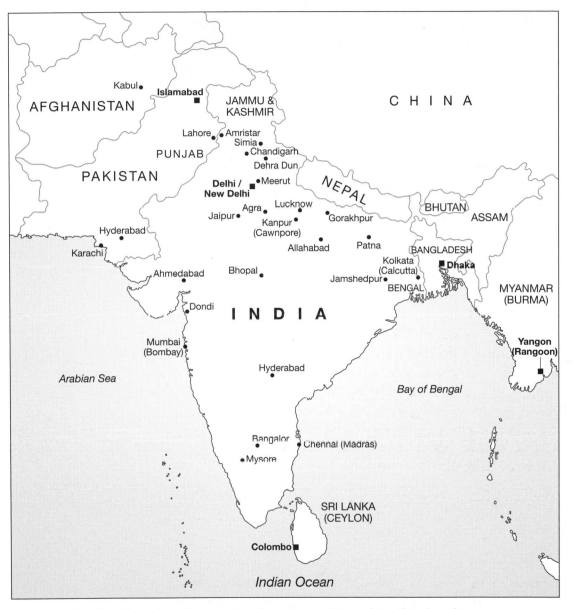

A map of India showing the main places mentioned in this book

INTRODUCTION

From East India Company to Raj

In the mid-1730s, so the story goes, a schoolboy called Robert Clive truanted from school and climbed to the top of the church steeple in the Shropshire town of Market Drayton. Once there, he sat on the weather vane and shouted down gleefully at the passers-by. Thirty years later, this dare-devil younger son of a small landowner was an MP, fabulously rich and in 1772 was made Lord Lieutenant of Shropshire. How had he managed this? The answer, quite simply, was 'India'.

HOW AND WHY DID THE BRITISH BECOME INVOLVED IN INDIA?

The British first became involved in India because of trade. They were not the only people, however, to want a share of India's cotton and calico, muslins, chintzes, pepper, indigo and spices. By 1740 the Dutch, French and Portuguese, as well as the British, had established trading stations in India.

The Dutch and English companies depended on private finance; the Portuguese and French companies were funded by their respective governments. The various trading companies regularly took gold and silver as well as wool and metals to their company 'factories', which were really fortified trading stations, and almost always situated on the coast. There they were exchanged for goods the Europeans wanted. In the early days, spices dominated the Indian–European trade; by the end of the eighteenth century, Indian textiles had overtaken spices as the 'must have' commodity back in Europe.

What part did the East India Company play in the British economy?

All British trade with India was run by the East India Company, based in Leadenhall Street in the City of London. Its operations were governed by a charter of 1698, which allowed it to have a **monopoly of trade** with India in return for certain financial restrictions and restrictions on the sort of goods that could be traded.

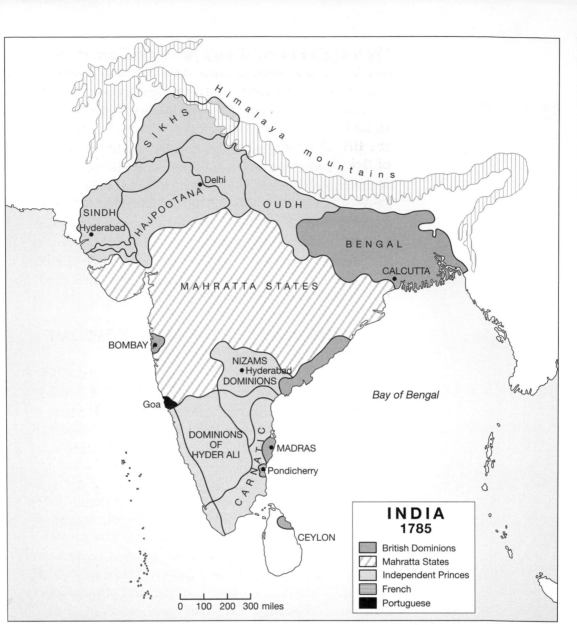

Outline map of India showing the controlling powers and the European trading stations c.1785

More importantly, the charter allowed for East India Company affairs to be debated in Parliament. So right from the beginning, there was parliamentary interest in what British merchants were doing in India. There was some measure of control, too: Parliament could always refuse to renew the East India Company's Charter.

KEY LETTER

Part of a letter written in 1698, from the directors of the East India Company in London to their merchants in India:

Your chintz from Ahmedabad, your chintz from Seringapatam and in general all the coloured goods are profitable commodities, whereof send large quantities, taking care the cloth be good.

Company shareholders lived mainly in London and the south-east, and were an important part of a complex system of international trade, focused on London. In the 20 years before Robert Clive arrived in India, the East India Company was a stable, but unspectacular, part of the British economic scene. It handled about 13 per cent of British imports and 5 per cent of Britain's exports. It paid its shareholders around 7 per cent annually. However, the East India Company had an importance far beyond that of keeping its shareholders happy. Its importance lay in the way in which the Company conducted first, its commercial business in India, and later the development of this commercial business into political power.

How did the East India Company organise its commercial business in India?

Throughout most of the eighteenth century the British, like other European traders, were more influenced by India than influencing it. It was the Indian people, finance, products and circumstances that dictated how trade and commerce developed. They, and not the Europeans, created the framework within which trade was possible. It had to be like this. India was not a vast continent inhabited by natives anxious to trade precious commodities for a handful of beads. On the contrary, India had a sophisticated and complex system of government, dominated by the Mughal Empire (see page 7) but containing some smaller kingdoms, all of which had well-established trading links, routes and patterns within India, Asia and beyond. British merchants had to work with the systems they found in India.

Trading stations

The East India Company's trading stations in Bombay, Calcutta and Madras acted as secure bases from which the East India Company operated. Each of the Company's trading stations had its own President, or Governor. He was advised by his Council, made up of senior and very experienced merchants. Beneath this council were other Senior Merchants who hadn't quite made it to the Council, then the Junior Merchants, then the **Factors**

(see page 7)

KEY TERMS

Factor An agent of a company, usually buying and selling on commission for that company.

Writer A clerk, usually engaged in writing up invoices, checking payments, ordering goods and, in the days before photocopiers, a lot of copying out where duplicates were needed of anything.

and finally the **Writers**. It was a hierarchical society where everyone knew his place. Membership of this hierarchy was highly prized within British professional and commercial families. Indeed, to become a Writer (the lowliest person within this structure) a young man, who had to be at least sixteen years of age, had to be sponsored by one of the Directors of the East India Company. So he, or his family, had to be known to them.

The Company's trading stations at Bombay (now known as Mumbai), Calcutta (now Kolkata) and Madras (now Chennia), each had its own army. These armies were intended to protect the interests of the East India Company. So within the trading stations lived soldiers, surgeons and chaplains too. Other Europeans, not working for the East India Company, managed to live under the Company's protection. Shopkeepers, lawyers and jewellers were among those living in Calcutta in the eighteenth century. Life in the trading stations was anything but narrow and strait-laced. Men with a mind for it could spend their spare time at wild parties, dancing, gambling and getting roaring drunk. Indeed, they must have thought, what else was there to do?

Many young men like Robert Clive, recruited by the Company to be Writers, died on the journey to India. Once there, still more succumbed to malaria, cholera and other tropical diseases against which they had no protection. Some lived out difficult lives suffering from the ills of the climate, the distance from home and the tedium of the job. But for others, it was very different.

India was the place, and the East India Company the organisation, where young men with daring, bravery, cunning, greed and a great deal of luck, were able to make their fortunes, as the story of Robert Clive shows. In the eighteenth century, a letter from London to India could take as long as six months to arrive. This gave the Company men in India a pretty free hand to make on-the-spot decisions. They had come to India to make their fortune and they acted accordingly.

Private trade and private fortunes

Every single person entering the East India Company as a Writer had to sign a covenant with the Company by which they agreed to 'good behaviour' and 'fair dealings'. This must have been very loosely interpreted! Hundreds of men employed by the East India Company as Writers, Factors and Merchants did a lot of work on the side. Using the protection of the Company, they built up complex 'private' trade networks, working in a totally private capacity and for their own, not the Company's, profit. They usually worked with Indians, who were experienced in working with established Indian trading networks, and who supplied local knowledge and considerable capital. These private enterprises extended to having a private merchant fleet based in Calcutta and to private trading, not only within India, but also around the coast and eastwards to China.

As the East India Company's influence expanded, so did the unofficial activities of its members. By 1763, for example, private involvement in Bengal's trade amounted to over £500,000 – more than the East India Company's annual profit!

There can be some excuse for what might seem to be something of a racket. Quite simply, the East India Company did not pay its employees enough to live on, and they had to make money in other ways. This money wasn't only made through private trade. To be a Company employee meant that relationships with the Indians with whom they did business had to be established and had to be positive. The Indians made sure of this (it was in their interests, too) and showered East India Company employees with gifts, as was the Mughal custom. A House of Commons select committee worked out that, in the years 1757–69, East India Company employees received, in Bengal alone, over £2 million in presents. And that was only the gifts they had admitted to receiving!

Why did commercial involvement in India become political?

In 1767, the East India Company's secretary assured the House of Commons that the Company was only interested in trade with India: 'It is commercial interest we look for' he assured MPs, who were growing worried at the extent of the Company's involvement in the subcontinent. Ten years later, the Secretary to the

KEY TERM

Nabob A British man who has returned to Britain with a fortune made in India.

KEY QUOTES

The first Mughal Emperor, **Babur** controlled a large part of Northern India by 1530. This is how one of his courtiers describes how Indian noble families flocked to support the Mughals:

> *In the very truth, the greater part of the inhabitants of this world are like a flock of sheep; wherever one goes, the others immediately follow.*

A Portuguese missionary who met **Akbar** recorded:

> *Akbar (Babur's grandson, who reigned 1556–1605) was interested and curious to learn about many things, and possessed an intimate knowledge, not only of military and political matters, but of many of the mechanical arts. In his eagerness for knowledge, he tried to learn everything at once, like a hungry man trying to swallow his food in a single gulp.*

An English traveller who visited Akbar's court wrote:

> *He has writers who by turns set down everything in writing which he does, so that there is nothing that happens in his lifetime which is not noted, not even his going to the lavatory. All this is done for one purpose: that when he dies these writings of all his actions and speeches which are set down may be recorded in the chronicles.*

KEY ERA

The era of the '**Great Mughals**' refers to the time between 1530 and 1707, when five Emperors, Humayan, Akbar, Jehangir, Shah Jehan and Aurangzeb, took the Mughal Empire to its greatest heights in extent,

Treasury noted that the whole idea of the East India Company exercising political power in India was 'absurd and preposterous'. Yet the Company did increasingly exercise political power within India, whether they denied it or not, and whether they liked it or not. How did this come about? There was one main reason: the decline of the Mughal Empire. The slow collapse of this once-great empire created a power vacuum and, as power slipped from Mughal hands, Indian claimants warred with each other at the regional level of politics and government. Commerce and trade inevitably suffer when there is political instability and this was the case in India. In attempting to protect their trading interests, the East India Company was drawn into Indian politics and began to exercise political power.

How powerful was the Mughal Empire?

The first Mughal ruler to invade India was **Babur**, who in 1504 held Kabul (in Afghanistan) and used it as a base from which to direct raids into northern India. By the time of his death in 1530, Babur was in control of a large area of northern India, including Delhi. His descendants continued his policy of conquest until, at its height in about 1660, the empire extended throughout most of present-day Afghanistan, Pakistan and all but the southernmost part of India.

Under the Mughals, India was not only the heart of a great Islamic empire, but also a centre of Islamic culture and learning. The courts of the five '**Great Mughals**' were luxurious places, sparkling with the richness of jewels and precious metals; they were, too, places of patronage for poets and musicians, artists and architects. A Mughal court – particularly under **Akbar** – was always on the move. This vast, luxurious tented city accommodating some 250,000 people, with all the 'buildings' of a royal palace including a harem and mosque, moved steadily throughout the empire, supporting and hunting, conquering and re-conquering.

The Mughals were Muslims, and yet most of their people were Hindu, with completely different beliefs and customs. These differences are explained in detail in Chapter 7 pages 107–18 (also pages 17–18), but here it is sufficient to realise that, in the seventeenth and eighteenth centuries, Hindu and Muslim could and did live peacefully together.

The Emperor Akbar (ruled 1556–1605) was perhaps the foremost of the 'Great Mughals' in making strenuous efforts to prevent religious discord. Perhaps most importantly, one of his many wives was a Hindu princess from Rajputana. She was particularly favoured because it was her son who succeeded Akbar. This marriage was not only a clever move in religious terms, but it bought the loyalty of the fierce Rajput warriors for the next hundred or so years. Akbar encouraged calm and reasoned debate on religious matters; he promoted leading Hindus to high positions in the Mughal civil service; he abolished the *jizya* – a hated poll tax levied on all non-muslims; he abolished the tax on pilgrimages to Hindu shrines and, indeed, positively encouraged the building of Hindu temples and the holding of Hindu festivals.

The Mughal emperors used the *mansabdar* system to generate revenue and to help control their vast empire. The emperor would grant land to a *mansabdar*

This seventeenth-century painting shows the magnificence of the court of the Emperor Akbar. Here, Akbar is receiving a copy of the Akbarnama, a history of his reign written on his orders, from his biographer Abdul-azi

and, with the land, the right to collect revenue. In return, the *mansabdar* had to promise to provide the emperor with soldiers in time of war. The greater the size of the land granted, the greater the number of soldiers the *mansabdar* had to promise. These agreements could be revoked at any time by the emperor and were non-

The Mughal Emperor Farrukhsiyar (1701–1719). A few years after this picture was painted his most senior official, Husain Ali Khan, plotted against the emperor and had him strangled

hereditary. This gave the emperor a large degree of control. Strong emperors, like Akbar, were able to move *mansabdars* around the empire every three to four years, promoting the able by making them larger grants of land and demoting the less proficient by granting them smaller areas of land from which to obtain revenue.

This system worked well when an emperor was strong and local officials trustworthy. However, a weak emperor was in trouble. Corrupt village leaders held back revenue for themselves; *mansabdars* retained revenue, refused to provide soldiers for the emperor, and sought power for themselves and their followers. This was one of the main reasons for the collapse of the Mughal Empire. In the twelve years after the death of the Emperor Aurangzeb in 1707, there were ten successive emperors, whereas in the previous 181 years there had only been six.

This weakness at the top led to the rise of faction and the increase in power of local rulers. In the north the Jats and Sikhs, and in the west, the Marathas firmly resisted Mughal attempts to govern them. In the south, the ruler

RICHES GALORE

When Clive was installed as Governor of Bengal, he received an immediate personal fortune of £234,000. He was made a *mansabdar* and received lands south of Calcutta worth £30,000 a year. At the age of 32 he had become one of the richest men in Britain.

THE SIEGE OF ARCOT 1751

Robert Clive was besieged in Arcot when it was surrounded by a vastly superior French and Indian force. Clive defended Arcot for 50 days until help came. The siege greatly added to Clive's reputation as a charismatic leader. It also marked the beginning of the decline of French power in India and a turning point in the fortunes of the East India Company.

of Hyderabad ruled over a large, virtually independent state. As the power of the Mughal emperors weakened, more and more small-scale wars were fought throughout the eighteenth century as rival Indian princes battled for supremacy.

WHAT WAS THE REACTION OF THE EAST INDIA COMPANY?

In this complex and complicated situation, the East India Company was another player, with a different set of interests. Their main interest was, of course, trade, but there were other imperatives.

A series of European wars between the French and the British spilled over into India, where the French were traders too. Both sides found allies in rival Indian princes and their factions, and so were drawn into India's political struggles.

The first open confrontation occurred in southern India, where Dupleix and the French East India Company had built up quite a power base. Both the British and French companies wanted their own nominee as *nawab*, or ruler, of Arcot, the area around Madras. At the end of a long struggle, Robert Clive installed the man the British wanted and supported him with arms and cash. Clive had outmanoeuvred the French, leaving them with only a few small enclaves in southern India.

The French and British again backed different factions in the struggle for control of Bengal, which had been a Mughal stronghold. Clive's intervention was again successful and he defeated the *nawab* Siraj-ud-Daula at the **Battle of Plassey** in 1757. Here he was helped by a combination of disgruntled soldiers, landholders and influential merchants whose commercial profits were closely linked to those of the East India Company. Commercial interests were, even at this level, involved and no Indian merchant would be likely to support a side that would not deal well with him afterwards.

When Clive returned to India from England in 1765, the Mughal Emperor, weak and with his forces defeated by the British at Buxar, had conferred on the East India Company administrative rights over Bengal, Bihar and

For much of the 18th century, many Englishmen in India had Indian wives and mixed socially with Indians. This painting shows William Palmer with his two Indian wives, daughter and two of his sons, together with three other women. It was painted by Francesco Renaldi in 1786.

Orissa, a region of roughly 25 million people with an annual revenue of 40 million rupees. The Emperor made the Company his *Diwan*, or chief financial manager. With Clive installed as the first British Governor of Bengal, the British were established as a major political force in India. So it seemed that the East India Company had slipped into some of the Mughal Emperors' shoes, taking up the revenue administration for Bengal, the richest province in India.

The British in India continued to gain power and influence over local Indian rulers. The Company was immensely wealthy; it could strike hard bargains with local merchants; it loaned money to minor Indian rulers and, when they defaulted on repayments, took over running their states.

THE BATTLE OF PLASSEY 1757

The *nawab* Siraj-ud-Daula, supported by the French, was intent on causing trouble for the East India Company. Robert Clive led a force of about 1000 European and 2000 Indian soldiers against him. Clive found Siraj-ud-Daula at Plassey, on the banks of the River Bhagirathi, where he was leading a force of 50,000 men. A rainstorm soaked the Siraj's artillery powder. Clive's men had kept their powder dry, and were able easily to defeat the Siraj's forces. Robert Clive was left in charge of Bengal.

KEY COMMENT

Robert Clive wrote this about Calcutta in 1765 when he was Governor-General:

I will pronounce Calcutta to be one of the most wicked places in the universe. Corruption, and a lack of principle seem to have possessed the minds of all the civil servants; by frequent bad examples they are grown callous, greedy and extravagant beyond belief.

HOW DID THE BRITISH GOVERNMENT REACT?

Back in Britain there was considerable concern about the activities of the East India Company. It was no longer simply a trading company. It had a huge private army and was actively involved in administering a large amount of the Indian subcontinent. It was answerable to no one but its shareholders.

The British government tried to achieve some sort of control. In 1784 it set up a Board of Control, based in London, to oversee the Company's affairs. The government also created the post of Governor-General for the Company who was answerable to the Board of Control. To some extent this worked. In 1788 the Governor-General, Warren Hastings, was ordered to appear before the House of Lords, charged with ruthlessness and corruption. After a trial lasting nine years he was finally acquitted, but that didn't stop concerns about the activities of the East India Company rumbling on.

REBELLION! MAY 1857

Trouble was to hit the East India Company in May 1857. A rising among the Indian soldiers of the Company's Bengal Army turned into a widespread rebellion involving a number of different grievances.

One of the most significant grievances concerned the conditions of service of the soldiers in the Bengal army. In 1856 the General Enlistment Order imposed the same conditions on sepoys serving in the Bengal, Bombay and Madras armies. All sepoys were expected to serve wherever the East India Company decided to send them, even abroad. At a stroke this removed a privilege from the sepoys in the Bengal army – the payment of *batta,* an allowance payable if they served 'abroad' i.e. outside of territory held by the East India Company.

The trigger for the rebellion appeared to come from the cartridges issued for use with the new Enfield rifle that was adopted in 1857. The rifles' cartridges were rumoured to be greased with tallow containing both pork and beef fat. As beef fat was repugnant to Hindus, and pork fat was offensive to Muslims, the sepoys refused to use them. The offending cartridges were quickly withdrawn, but the damage had been done. All existing cartridges were suspect as was virtually all official government issue, including such items as flour and cooking oil. A particularly insensitive handling of the situation in Meerut, an important garrison town about 37 miles (60 kilometres) from Delhi, started the conflagration. There, the garrison commander court-martialled 85 Indians for refusing to use suspect cartridges and publicly humiliated them. The following day, 10 May, the sepoys mutinied, began massacring Europeans and marched to Delhi, gathering support as they went. Once in Delhi, they pledged support to the somewhat bemused elderly Mughal Emperor who had 'ruled' harmlessly from the Red Fort for over 20 years with neither subjects nor troops. Mutiny spread quickly throughout the Bengal army. Within weeks most of the garrisons in the north-west provinces and Oudh were in rebel hands, the British officers, their wives and children slaughtered.

The rebellion wasn't simply a military one. Civilian rebellion spread rapidly across the Gangetic plain as whole areas of British authority collapsed. There was no carefully planned, orchestrated rebellion. It was far more a series of localised responses to separate and different fears of new influences and changing patterns of authority. The revolt spread down the Ganges valley to Agra, Lucknow and Kanpur. British forces and their families were taken prisoner and murdered. As word of the murders spread, British reprisals were terrible. Entire villages were torched; unarmed Indians and even domestic servants were attacked, mutilated and murdered. Fear and hatred destroyed the bridges that many had so carefully built between Indian and British. Gradually order was restored, but it took until December 1857 before the key strategic points along the Ganges valley were reoccupied and a further five months before all resistance was stamped out.

It is important to remember that huge areas of India were untouched by this rebellion. Beyond the Gangetic plain and parts of central India, there were very few disturbances in 1857–8. Bengal, Madras and Bombay were quiet. Even where there were disturbances, there are many instances of Indians loyally defending the British for whom they worked. Indeed, in the Punjab, Sikh princes worked with the British to restore order.

The British government spent £36m restoring order. This was a full year's worth of Indian revenue. It was hardly surprising that, in August 1858, the British parliament passed the Government of India Act, transferring all rights that the East India Company had enjoyed on Indian soil directly to the British Crown.

The troubles of 1857 demonstrated several things.

- Britain was the only power that was capable of maintaining law and order throughout India.
- British authority could be established, and re-established, by calling on armed forces from Britain to support those stationed in India.
- British authority could only be maintained by relying on a network of Indians who either sympathised with the British or who were willing to cooperate with them until better times came.

THE BRITISH RAJ

The Government of India Act meant that Queen Victoria became Queen of India as well as of the United Kingdom, and India's Governor-General became her Viceroy (see Curzon page 31) as well as the government's chief executive in India. Just as in the United Kingdom, the position of the monarch was buttressed by a hierarchical structure of hereditary nobles and honours, so in India a similar structure was created.

With very few exceptions, the 500 or so Indian princes had remained loyal to the British throughout the Great Rebellion. In British eyes, such loyalty deserved recognition and reward. Existing treaties with India's princes were to be scrupulously maintained and the hated 'doctrine of lapse' whereby princedoms without a direct heir 'lapsed' to British control was abandoned. A royal order of Indian knights was created; India's princes were grouped and stratified according to status. Status was, of course, dependent upon size of territory, but also on good government and charitable works, and a prince's status was confirmed by a multitude of protocols, amongst which was the right to insist on a specific number of gun salutes.

In 1876, on the advice of her Prime Minister, Benjamin Disraeli, Queen Victoria announced to Parliament that her Indian subjects were 'happy under My rule and loyal to My throne'. Henceforward, she was to adopt the title 'Empress of India' which, for her Indian subjects, translated as 'Kaiser-i-Hind'. In January 1877, in a vast tented assembly outside Delhi, this new Imperial role was confirmed by most of India's princes and Indians of importance and influence.

However, the pomp and splendour concealed a number of issues that had to be addressed, as the twentieth century got under way.

The British were beginning to ask some fundamental questions:

- How was India to be administered and financed?
- What was India's worth to Britain?
- What was Britain's duty to India and the Indian people?

Other, equally fundamental, questions were being asked by the Indian people:

- What should their attitude be to the new British rulers? Should Indians cooperate with the British Raj? Should they oppose it?
- Should Indian people accept or reject the new opportunities offered by the British Raj or stand aloof from them?

There were no right answers to these questions. They were answered in different ways, by different people, at different times.

SUMMARY QUESTIONS

1 What problems faced the Indian people as they tried to cope with the impact of Europeans on their sub-continent?

2 Outline the stages by which most of India came under the control of the British Crown.

3 The Victorian historian, Sir John Seeley, said that the British 'seem to have conquered and peopled half the world in a fit of absence of mind'. How far do you think he was correct as far as India was concerned?

CHAPTER 1

Living in the Raj: India in 1900

Indian society was complex and of infinite variety. Basic to the way in which Indian society operated was the caste system. Only Hindus lived out their lives within the caste system, but as Hindus made up about 70 per cent of India's population of around 300 million in 1900, obviously it had a tremendous impact on society in the subcontinent. Added to this rich variety was the British Raj. By 1900, around 100,000 British people lived in India. They worked as civil servants, administrators, engineers, policemen and soldiers. Together with their wives and children they created a separate class that, with few notable exceptions, was determined to remain so. This chapter looks at the ways in which Indians and British lived out their lives at the beginning of the twentieth century and at their attitudes towards each other.

INDIAN SOCIETY: STRUCTURE AND ASSUMPTIONS

How did the caste system operate?

The majority of Indians were born into, and lived out their days within, a hierarchical system of caste. Their place in the social order was determined by the accident of birth – the caste into which they had been born. Caste society ranked in order, from high to low, whole groups of people, not individuals. No one could leave the caste into which they had been born unless they were literally out-caste, and then they had no place in society. Marriage took place within the caste and so no one could change one caste for another. All social relationships, those between, for example, men and women, relatives, neighbours, employers and employed, were pre-determined by caste and learned from childhood. However, as the twentieth century progressed, in some areas and within some societies, the caste system did begin to become flexible.

The assumptions underlying the caste system were those of purity and pollution. Certain substances were considered to be religiously polluting (human and animal waste, for example, dead bodies and carcasses and anything associated with them, like leather) and so the closer whole groups were to such substances, the lower they were in the caste system. Some people, such as women during childbirth, became temporarily polluted and had to be purified. Others, because of their occupation, could never be completely purified and so, in order to protect the purity of the caste above them, the castes had to be kept as separate as possible. There were strict rules, too, on who could touch whom. Those at the bottom of the hierarchy, like scavengers, were literally untouchable.

Although this caste system was one of separation, it was also one of interdependence. Everyone needed the support of those above and below them in the system – even the work of the untouchables was essential to the smooth running of society. And so a system of patron–client relationships between families was established, often existing over many generations. A blacksmith, for example, needed a landowner to work for, just as the landowner needed someone to make his ploughs, and they both needed someone to take away human waste.

Varna is the basic four-caste system described in Hindu scriptures. This consists of **Brahmins** (priests), **Kshatriyas** (warriors), **Vaishyas** (traders) and **Shudras** (cultivators). In practice, most Indians experienced caste within the *jati*, which were essentially local groups with a known social order that operated between and within the four main caste groups.

This is a family of 'untouchables' in front of their house

What was the importance of religion?

Caste, as you have seen, was intimately intertwined with the Hindu religion. But religion, whether it was Hindu or Muslim, Sikh or Jain, was a vital bonding force between people and groups. It determined value systems and provided a framework for dress, diet and social customs as well as the rituals associated with a particular form of belief. As well, therefore, as being a binding force, religion in India, as well as in the rest of the world, was also divisive, setting different groups of people apart from each other, often in mutual misunderstanding and distrust. It is not surprising that such a powerful force played a dominant part in twentieth-century Indian politics, as change inevitably altered the relationships between the different communities.

The majority of Indians in 1900 were Hindu (about 70 per cent), as they had been when the first Europeans set foot on Indian soil. Other religions were brought to India with waves of invaders and migrants. Muslims formed the largest minority religion (around 20 per cent) and in some parts of the subcontinent, mostly in the north-west and east, they were in the majority. In the north-west, Muslims still tended to hold influential positions, while in the area around Bengal, Muslims were more likely to be found forming the peasant class. There were fewer Muslims in southern India, except in Hyderabad which had been a stronghold of the Mughal Empire.

Sikhs and Christians were the other two sizeable minority groups. Sikhs formed a highly localised group, mainly in the Punjab, and grew out of the interaction between Hindu and Muslim in the sixteenth and seventeenth centuries. In the far south of India there was an ancient denomination of Christians who claimed St Thomas as their founder, but most of the Christians in India were those who had been converted by missionaries in the nineteenth century.

As you read this book, you will see just what a powerful force religion was in India. In their struggle towards independence different groups and communities struggled to adjust identities and imperatives in a changing political framework. Different caste groups, for example, organised themselves and mobilised their members for political action; Hindu temples became focal points of political activity. To proclaim that certain political policies and plans endangered Islam was a powerful motivating force for Muslims to engage in political action, and here the local clerics showed considerable organisational skills.

Agriculture

For most Indians, life went on as it had done for decades, with agriculture as the basis of their lives. The actual crops varied from area to area, as you would expect over such a huge subcontinent. Rice was the basic crop, but in the drier areas wheat, barley, millet and maize were grown. Most farmers grew for their own basic needs and to enable them to do a little bartering. More enterprising farmers grew indigo, opium and cotton for the export market, although this remained pretty static during the eighteenth and early nineteenth centuries.

The ending of the East India Company's monopoly on trade with India in 1833, and the establishing of the British Raj less than 30 years later, had a dynamic effect on agriculture, although it was not always to the benefit of the Indians. An influx of British and European merchants, traders and planters led to the development of vast, new tea and coffee plantations. In 1851, for example, there had been just one tea plantation in British India, producing 200,000 pounds of tea per year. By 1871 this had risen to some 295 tea plantations, producing over 6 million pounds of tea a year.

After the Great Rebellion, the British first decided to destroy the Indian landowning class, the *taluqdars*, by confiscating their property but later there was a change of policy. At a glittering *durbar* held in Lucknow in October 1859, Lord Charles John Canning, India's first Viceroy, conferred special property contracts on the assembled *taluqdars*. These contracts, called *sanads*, restored their lands to them in perpetuity. In this way the Raj hoped to build up a loyal, landowning class. In this they were largely successful. Indeed, in 1861 the *taluqdars* of Oudh organised themselves into the British Indian Association – a loyal, conservative institution whose primary aim was to support the British Raj.

Agriculture and industry were in many instances closely linked, as was shown by the indigo industry. Indigo was grown by farmers and then manufactured into indigo dye. The demand for the dye, and the rate at which it could be produced, clearly had an impact on the demand for raw indigo from the farmer. British and Europeans moved in quickly on the indigo industry in Bihar and Bengal, creating a demand for indigo, but at the same time creating and perpetuating working conditions so terrible that the years 1859–60 saw the first ever strike by Indians against British management. The resulting Indigo Commission found in favour of the Indian peasants and the British owners had to amend their practices.

Industry

Few Indians worked in industry, and the industries that did exist (mainly iron, cotton, jute and coal) were on a small scale. Although the first cotton mills opened in Bombay in the mid-nineteenth century, most Indian industry was carried on at home within the general framework of the village. Potters and weavers, jewellery makers and blacksmiths, all provided for the general needs of the villagers with a little left over. Even in 1939, there were only 2 million industrial workers in the whole of India.

However, the 1850s saw a shift in the way cotton, India's premier industry, was manufactured because of the introduction of European-style cotton factories. By 1900 there were about 200 mills in India, mostly in Bombay and Ahmedabad, with over 5 million spindles producing around 500 million pounds of cotton thread, about half of which was sold overseas. The production of cotton cloth was on a much smaller scale and only met about 10 per cent of India's home demands. The rest of the home demand was met by foreign imports – mostly cotton cloth manufactured in Lancashire from Indian-produced thread. The British unashamedly supported the Lancashire cotton industry to the detriment of the Indian industry, making India subordinate to the needs of Lancashire. For example, in 1879 Viceroy Lytton, in the face of opposition from his whole Council, removed all import duties on Lancashire cotton cloth allowing it to flood the Indian market at a time when the Indian cotton industry desperately needed support and the people were suffering a famine. The significance of the situation in which the Indian cotton industry found itself was used later by Gandhi (see pages 80–83) to great effect.

British 'victory' in the Great Rebellion and subsequent transfer of power from the East India Company to the British Crown resulted in a great increase in British and European capital investment in Indian agriculture and industry. Victory convinced hitherto nervous investors that the British could, and would, continue to control and contain any further rebellion and that the British Empire in India was built on sound foundations.

Trade and communication

Trade was important and, as you read in the Introduction, always had been in India, from the time of the Mughal Empire to that of the East India Company. There was a great deal of internal trade, using the network of great rivers; a coastal trade, with inshore ships sailing up and down the coast from port to port; and an international trading network. Internal trade consisted mainly of foodstuffs and cloth. It is difficult to distinguish coastal trade from the international, but in the nineteenth century the main comodities that were taken down to the coast were opium, indigo and cloth (especially silk, but also cotton).

Trade, and particularly trade in the products of industry and agriculture, benefited from a good transport and communication network. The metalled road that was built by the British (using Indian labour) before the Rebellion, and which linked Calcutta and Delhi, was continued afterwards to Peshawar. By 1859, 432 miles (695 kilometres) of railway lines had been laid down; by 1900 there were 25,000 miles (40,234 kilometres) of track, snaking across the sub-continent. However, all track, engines, carriages and other equipment were made in Britain, where the market of the steel companies in the Midlands was constantly expanding, thanks to the demands of India.

The telegraph system had proved its worth during the Great Rebellion, and this was further expanded afterwards. By 1900, twenty thousand miles (more than 32,000 kilometres) of telegraph wires criss-crossed the sub-continent.

These newly developing industries, subordinated though they were to British industry, did provide thousands of new employment opportunities for Indian workers.

WHAT WAS LIFE LIKE FOR THE BRITISH IN INDIA?

It is impossible to underestimate the impact of the Great Rebellion and the level of racial distrust it raised between the British white population of India and the Indians themselves. The bitter legacy of murder and mutilation, of atrocities committed by both sides, poisoned relationships for decades.

Shocked at what they perceived as disloyalty and ingratitude, the British response was to separate themselves from the Indian people. In doing so they created what was a separate ruling elite. This separation of rulers from the ruled was to lead to terrible problems as both sides tried to reach new understandings as the twentieth century progressed.

Calcutta Calcutta, the administrative capital of British India, was the magnet that drew anyone who wanted to be part of smart society. It was here that the British could live in a more lavish style than they could have afforded in Britain on the same money. When the Viceroy was in residence and the Calcutta season in full swing, there were balls, dances, parties and receptions every night. And always it was the Indians who prepared the food, waited at table, served the drinks, washed up and swept up afterwards.

A separate society

In the great cities of Bombay, **Calcutta** and Madras, wealthy Raj officials, as well as bankers, lawyers and merchants along with their families, lived in the great eighteenth-century houses that had once belonged to officials of the East India Company. They were looked after by an army of Indian servants. Those not so well off lived in bungalows, though still with Indian servants to do the cleaning and cooking, and single men usually shared a house and servants. In the latter half of the nineteenth century, new towns and suburbs called 'civil lines' and 'camps' were built for British officials and their families. They were deliberately built with wide streets along which a regiment could move swiftly to put down any 'trouble'.

Children were looked after by an *ayah*, an Indian nurse, until they were old enough to be sent off to boarding schools in England. The opening of the Suez canal in 1869, important as it was for political and military reasons, did shorten the journey 'home' and further encouraged the British servants of the Crown to bring their wives out to India and rear their children there. Holidays could now be spent in London and relatives could be visited. To live and work in India was no longer viewed as exile.

The distrust and suspicion with which most of the British in India viewed the Indians led to the breakdown of the relationships between the races. After the Great Rebellion, far fewer British men took Indian wives or (as far as we can tell) mistresses. They preferred the security of a British wife. Ships travelling from Britain, nicknamed 'fishing fleets', carried considerable numbers of young single women, more hopeful of finding a husband than visiting the faded glories of Mughal India.

The British formed a separate section in a society that was divided by caste. However, within British society there were many hierarchical divisions. Every one knew exactly where they stood in the social pecking order: with whom they could take tea and with whom they could be the ones to speak first. Indeed, the government published a 'warrant of precedence', with the Viceroy at the top and the Sub-Deputy Opium Agent at the bottom. This rigid ordering of society continued in India long after education and war had dissolved such barriers in Britain. The privations of war did not hit British society in India in the same way it did in the UK, and it was perceived, perhaps subconsciously, that the maintenance of barriers would provide continuing security.

The Calcutta Golf Club, 1910

Simla

In the hot season, every British person who could afford it (and who hadn't taken advantage of the P&O shipping line and gone back to Britain for a break) moved to the hills where it was cooler and life could be a little more relaxed. The Viceroy and the higher departments of state moved to Simla in the foothills of the Himalayas. With them went the leaders of the business community and everyone whose status made contact with the Viceroy in a social situation acceptable. Simla was cut off from the plains by 58 miles (93 kilometres) of poor roads and from Calcutta by 1000 miles (1609 kilometres). Other similar settlements were known as hill stations and were often even more remote. Indeed, this remoteness made the hill stations attractive. There the British could begin to enjoy themselves: the men played polo and went hunting; the women played tennis, badminton and croquet. There were balls and picnics. Whilst this might have been fun for the British, it served, in Indian eyes, to separate them even more from the people they governed. And the very business of government tended to be put on hold while the British enjoyed themselves.

Vera Birdwood described her life in India:

> We were looked after by Indian servants and we met a great many Indians, and some of us undoubtedly made a very close study of India and Indian customs. But once you stepped inside the home you were back in Cheltenham or Bath. We brought with us in our home lives almost exact replicas of the sort of life that upper-middle-class people lived in England at that time. Nearly everyone in official India sprang from precisely the same educational and cultural background. You went from bungalow to bungalow and you found the same sort of furniture, the same sort of dinner table set, the same kind of conversation. We read the same books, mostly imported by post from England, and I can't really say that we took an awful lot from India.

Many Englishwomen despaired of ever really being able to recreate their part of England in India and stories abounded of Indian servants using their toes as toast racks and being caught straining soup through their turbans.

Living close to the edge
Not all the British in India, however, were privileged. Among the less favoured were the missionaries, whose

poverty and desire to live among the Indians made them deeply suspect, and businessmen whose social origins were usually regarded as dubious. Anyone connected with the lower echelons of trade, such as a shopkeeper, was automatically barred from this hierarchical British society that had recreated itself in India.

Anglo-Indians were equally suspect. Numbering about 110,000 at the beginning of the twentieth century, they were accepted by neither the British nor the Indians. The nearest they came to polite British society was in church, where they were consigned to the lowliest pews, and on occasions when they were the recipients of dubious charitable gestures like children's Christmas parties. They identified themselves with Britain, referring to it as 'home' although they had never been there, dressing in European clothes and, in the case of women, trying to lighten their complexions with make-up. Yet it was this under-class that formed the backbone of labour on the railways and the postal and telegraph services. The British who so spurned them could not administer India without them.

WHAT WERE THE ATTITUDES OF THE BRITISH TOWARDS THE INDIAN PEOPLE?

Lord Curzon, the Viceroy in the years 1898–1905, had very decided views about the Indian princes and about the role of the British in India. In 1900 he said:

> *The Princes are unruly and ignorant and rather undisciplined schoolboys. What they want more than anything else is to be schooled by a firm hand. We sustain the Native States and Princes, not so much in the interests of the Princes themselves, who are often quite undeserving, but in the interests of the people. We are bound to train and discipline and control them and so fit them for the unique position which we have placed within their grasp.*

He was uneasy, too, about the handful of Indians who worked in the Indian Civil Service, complaining:

> *An increasing number of the higher posts that were meant, and ought to have been exclusively and specially reserved for Europeans, are being filched away by the superior wits of the native in the English examinations. I believe it to be the greatest peril with which our administration is confronted.*

Curzon clearly believed in the British purpose in India and would not be daunted:

(It is) because I believe in the future of India and the capacity of our own race to guide it to goals that it has never hitherto attained, that I keep courage and press forward.

You can read more about Curzon as Viceroy in the next chapter, pages 31–35.

Curzon's attitude was reflected by the poet **Rudyard Kipling**. Born in Bombay in 1865, Kipling worked in India as a journalist when he was a young man, before returning to England to live there permanently. He wrote the poem 'Take Up the White Man's Burden' in 1899. This is the first verse:

Take up the White Man's burden –
Send forth the best ye breed –
Go, bind your sons to exile
To serve your captives' need;
To wait, in heavy harness,
On fluttered folk and wild –
Your new-caught sullen peoples,
Half devil and half child.

Kipling also wrote about a **sepoy**, an Indian soldier, called Gunga Din:

Though I've belted you and flayed you,
By the livin' Gawd that made you,
You're a better man than I am, Gunga Din!

WHAT WERE THE ATTITUDES OF INDIANS TOWARDS THE BRITISH RAJ?

In many ways this is a very difficult question to answer. It is a question that arises time and time again as India moved towards independence in 1947. As you work through this book you will see that this question was answered by different people in different ways at different times.

In 1900, when the British Raj was at its height, it was very difficult for ordinary Indian people to be openly critical of those who ruled them. After all, the Raj did employ a great number of Indians, thus providing them with a roof over their heads and food on their tables, an occupation and, in some cases, the makings of a career structure. But it was an alien rule, not one chosen by the Indian people themselves and not one arising, as the Mughal Empire had, from their own culture. This alien culture brought with it the English language. This language itself, while providing a unifying element, carried words like 'democracy' and 'imperialism' and, more importantly, the concepts behind those words. Indeed, command of English was necessary for Indians to pass examinations, once they were allowed to enter them, that allowed access to the prestigious Indian Civil Service.

Indian children attending British-run schools usually had to wear British-style uniforms, learn British games and work from textbooks produced in England. One Indian who went to such a school later wrote:

> The school textbooks prescribed in British days had a strong imperialist flavour. I remember how many of us squirmed on being called upon to recite a poem about an English hero who was killed in India in a frontier skirmish:
>
> 'Let dusky Indians whine and kneel,
> An English lad must die.'
>
> I forget who was the author of this 'sensitive' piece.

(Quoted in Frank Moraes *Witness to an Era* pub 1973)

One wonders, too, at the lack of sensitivity of the teacher who insisted that this poem was recited by the pupils.

Nirad Chaudhuri, who wrote *The Autobiography of an Unknown Indian* which was published in 1951, recalled his childhood in Calcutta:

> I was influenced by the example of my parents who never went into any kind of society in which they were not treated as equals. I entertained no ambition whatever of hobnobbing with the English in India. As long as I lived in Calcutta I wore no article of English clothing and had none. In general, I disliked and despised the local English.

This attitude to the British was reflected in a leaflet widely circulated in Bengal in 1907:

Can these thieves really be our rulers? These thieves import a huge number of goods, made in their own country, and sell them in our markets, stealing our wealth and taking life from our people. Can those who steal the harvest from our fields and doom us to hunger, fever and plague really be our rulers? Can foreigners really be our rulers, foreigners who impose on us ever more taxes?

This view was reflected by the Indian academic, Dr Ashok Mitra:

Basically, the British were only interested in that kind of industrial growth which would help them back in Britain. They needed hessian – so they developed jute. They needed the railways to transport the raw materials to the coast, and so they built railways.

Some began to think that the time for change, radical change, had come. In 1907 Bal Gangadhar Tilak addressed the Indian National Congress, calling for a boycott of British goods and resistance to British rule. This is part of what he said:

At present, we are clerks and willing instruments of our own oppression in the hands of an alien government, and that government is ruling over us not by its innate strength but by keeping us in ignorance and blindness to the perception of this fact. Every Englishman knows that they are a mere handful in this country and it is the business of every one of them to befool you into believing that you are weak and they are strong.

This was a warning indeed that, with the new century, a change in the relationships between the Raj and the Indian people was going to come.

CONCLUSION

By 1900 the British were entrenched in India as a separate, élite class. Most of them regarded it as their right and their duty to rule India. Opinions differed as to whether this was in the interests of the Indians or the British. Among the Indians, many of whom owed their livelihood to the British, there was simmering discontent and growing resentment of what they were coming to regard as an alien rule.

SUMMARY QUESTIONS

1   To what extent can the Great Rebellion be seen as
    marking a turning point in British attitudes to the
    Indians? (You will need to refer to the Introduction as
    well as to information in this chapter.)

2   What similarities and what differences can you find
    between the attitudes of Lord Curzon and those of
    Rudyard Kipling?

3   What justification could have been given at the
    time for the lifestyle and attitudes of the British in
    Calcutta 'society'?

4   In this chapter there are four extracts from Indians
    themselves. What similar themes can you find in their
    attitudes to the Raj?

5   The Great Rebellion is sometimes called the
    Indian Mutiny and sometimes the War of Indian
    Independence. How appropriate, in your judgement,
    is each of these names?

CHAPTER 2

How was India governed in 1900?

By 1900 the British Raj was at its height. Not only did most British people agree with their queen that India was the 'jewel in the crown' but they regarded British rule in India as unassailable. Laws affecting India were made in the British Parliament and implementing these laws in India was managed efficiently. The Indian population were, by and large, cooperative and thousands of Indians worked for and with the British. Most British people, however, failed to realise just how much of their perceived control was an illusion, relying as it did on the lack of systematic opposition from the Indian people.

THE RAJ

The Viceroy, the Secretary of State and the Council of India

These institutions provided the 'top down' structure of the government of India. No other part of the British Empire had this structure and was paid this level of attention. This was partly because of the size of India, but also because of its importance to Britain. In Westminster, a Secretary of State for India, a political appointment, was responsible for government policy towards the subcontinent. The Viceroy was appointed by the British government at Westminster and so was also a political appointment. He was sent out to govern India as the personal representative of the monarch who, in 1900, was Queen Victoria. He was considered to be so important that not only was his salary twice that of the British prime minister, but he had a staff of 700 to make sure his working and living conditions befitted his status. Both were answerable to Parliament, where Indian affairs were debated and decisions made.

The Secretary of State was advised, guided and checked by a Council of India. This Council consisted of fifteen men, none of them Indian, but most of whom had had some experience of living and working in India in their younger days. This meant, of course, that their experience and therefore the advice they gave, was sometimes

---

KEY TERM

Viceroy This means, literally, deputy monarch. This is how the men who headed up the British government in India saw themselves.

KEY PEOPLE

Indian Viceroys 1898–1947

1898–1905	Lord Curzon
1905–10	Lord Minto
1910–16	Lord Hardinge
1916–21	Lord Chelmsford
1921–26	Lord Reading
1926–31	Lord Irwin
1931–36	Lord Willingdon
1936–43	Lord Linlithgow
1943–47	Lord Wavell
1947	Lord Mountbatten

alarmingly out-of-date. In quiet times this perhaps didn't matter too much. But when affairs in India moved swiftly, or threw up hitherto unsuspected challenges, the British response wasn't always appropriate. A good example of this is the partition of Bengal (see pages 33–34) which was brought about by Viceroy Curzon, entirely on his own initiative, in 1905.

There was frequently a tension between the Viceroy and the British government. Of course, a lot depended upon individual personalities and specific events, but this tension was built into the structure of the Raj. India and Indian affairs were open to the scrutiny of the British Parliament, and to the racial prejudices and political assumptions of Victorian (and later Edwardian and Georgian) England. As the Indian public became more literate and more politically aware, they were more ready to react openly to the ways in which the British Parliament handled Indian affairs. In India, the Viceroy had to consider Indian opinion and the views of his own officials; the government in Westminster had to ensure that the cost of governing India did not bankrupt the Treasury. These two different interests often clashed. As the man-on-the spot, the opinions and decisions of the Viceroy often prevailed over those of the Secretary of State, who was in theory his superior.

The army

By 1900 the British army in India was the strong-arm of the Raj. There were times when it was severely compromised, such as during the two world wars (see pages 52 and 131 but generally it could be called upon in any serious domestic emergency.

Dramatic reforms had taken place in the years after 1858. Under the 'old' East India Company, each **presidency** – Bengal, Bombay and Madras – had its own army. After the Great Rebellion, these separate armies were reorganised into one fighting force under the British Crown. The army was designed to prevent, as far as possible, any future rebellion.

- The ratio of Indian to British soldiers was reduced to between three to one and two to one.

- The British troops were given exclusive control over artillery and other 'scientific branches'.
- Indian soldiers were recruited only from those groups who had remained loyal to the British in the Great Rebellion. This automatically eliminated Bengalis, Biharis and **Marathas** and increased recruitment from Sikhs, Gurkhas, Pathans and Rajputs.
- Within each regiment, troops recruited from 'loyal' regions were mixed together.

Case Study: George Nathaniel Curzon, Viceroy of India 1898–1905

George Nathaniel Curzon was in many ways the most talented and best-suited man to be Viceroy of India. A study of the way in which he interpreted and carried out his role as Viceroy provides us with many insights into the ways in which the Raj operated in India at the turn of the last century.

Curzon, when he was a young man, had set his sights on becoming Viceroy of India and much of what he did was geared towards realising this ambition.

- He travelled extensively in the late 1880s and early 1890s and wrote a great deal, not only about India but also about its land frontiers and the great Asian steppes beyond. He visited Kabul, for example, and made friends with the amir, Abdur Rahman; he travelled over the Pamir mountains and through Chitral with Major Francis Younghusband as his guide.
- He developed a passion for Indian archaeology and culture, becoming something of an expert in both.
- He worked in Whitehall as under-secretary of state for India (1891–2) and in the Foreign Office (1892–5)

So when in 1898, Curzon finally achieved his ambition it might be expected that he would rule India with a degree of compassion and understanding. But this is what the historian **John Keay** has to say of him:

> *India's history fascinated him, and he was probably better informed about its languages and customs than any other Viceroy. But of its people as other than an administrative commodity and the decadent heirs of an interesting past he knew, and perhaps cared, little.*

Curzon was, in fact, an **imperialist** par excellence. He certainly had the traditional British view of India as the 'jewel in the imperial crown'. Indeed, he told the British Prime Minister Balfour, 'For as long as we rule India, we are the greatest power in the world.' Of Britain's role in India he had no doubt. Again, he told Balfour:

It will be well for England, better for India and best of all for the cause of progressive civilisation if it be clearly understood that we have not the smallest intention of abandoning our Indian possessions and that it is highly improbable that any such intention will be entertained by our posterity.

Efficiency was his watchword

Whatever Curzon's views, his single-mindedness in pursuing his aims cannot be doubted. Since the age of nineteen he wore a steel brace on his weak back and it has been suggested by the historian Stanley Wolpert that this may help to explain his compulsive drive, stamina and seemingly inexhaustible capacity for desk work. His watchword was 'efficiency' and he was determined to lead by example, spending, when he was in India, between ten and fourteen hours a day at his desk. While Viceroy he:

- appointed a special commission to study administrative procedures and, as a result of this, proposed office and procedural reforms that helped the administrative machine to run more smoothly
- created a new province, the North-West Frontier Province, in 1901 carving it out of the Punjab and bringing it directly under the control of the Viceroy
- moved control of the Indian railway from the Department of Public Works and brought it under the control of its own Board, enabling some 6000 more miles (9500 kilometres) of track to be laid by 1905
- appointed a director-general of archaeology responsible for unearthing, preserving and conserving India's cultural past. Curzon himself took a personal interest in restoring the Taj Mahal.

In some administrative reforms however, he failed. He wanted the governors of Bombay and Madras to send their weekly reports to him instead of to the Secretary of

KEY CONCEPT

Imperialism The extension of the power of a state by acquiring other territories and in doing so, creating an empire. This involved the subjugation of the people living there and their economic exploitation.

Almost all countries involved in imperialism defended it by explaining that it was their duty to bring civilisation to nations that had not yet experienced its benefits.

State for India in London, and he tried to administer every department and local government from his office.

Foreign policy: a success story?

Remember that, as a young man, Curzon had travelled extensively in the lands along India's land border, and it was here, as Viceroy, that he put his passion for efficiency and order to good use. He was also desperately afraid of Russian expansion into this wild and uncharted area. Curzon therefore acted decisively to secure the frontier.

- He created a buffer zone along the Afghan frontier that was patrolled by local militias under British command and with British subsidies and in 1901 transferred responsibility for this zone to the new North-West Frontier province.
- He directed British troop commanders, operating under the aegis of the Maharaja of Jammu, to push the frontier up to that of the Chinese Sinkiang, thus almost doubling the size of Kashmir.

BUT

- Claiming that the Dalai Lama was seeking Russian aid, Curzon convinced Whitehall of the necessity of taking over Tibet. This final 'tidying up' of India's land frontier in 1904 added Tibet to Britain's sphere of influence, but was accompanied by images of blood-soaked monks fumbling with hoes and flintlock pistols as they desperately tried to stave off the British invasion and the effects of the Gatling gun. It was not a good advertisement for imperialism and the British cabinet was beginning to feel a sense of alarm at Curzon's actions and reactions to threats, real and imagined.

The Partition of Bengal: Curzon's nemesis?

In 1905, against the counsel of all his British and Indian advisers, Curzon announced he was going to divide Bengal into two provinces: Eastern Bengal and Assam, which would have its capital in Dhaka, and Western Bengal, which would include the cities of Bihar and Orissa. Bengal, as it currently stood, was large, unruly, and difficult to administer. Efficiency and common sense, so Curzon reasoned, led inevitably to the decision he, and he alone, took to partition the province.

The Hindus immediately opposed this partition because it would create a province, Eastern Bengal, that was dominated by Muslims. Muslims, on the other hand, tended to support partition because it freed them from Hindu control, at least in one of the two new provinces.

Unsurprisingly, partition resulted in rioting and general unrest in Bengal and other parts of India. This unrest ranged from violence to more-or-less passive resistance.

A Bengali terrorist movement carried out a number of murders, and a boycott of British goods was started. A massive petition was presented to the Viceroy urging him to bring partition to an end, but to no avail.

At a stroke, Curzon had managed to spark a nationwide protest movement, introduce direct confrontation into British–Indian relationships, provoke sectarian conflict and suggest to the perceptive that partition was a 'solution' the British were not afraid to impose.

The end game

Curzon resigned as Viceroy within days of the partition of Bengal, but his resignation did not come because of the partition. It came as the result of an ongoing row Curzon was having with his Commander-in-Chief, Lord Kitchener. On the surface, the row concerned Kitchener's status on the Viceroy's Executive Council. Underlying this was the struggle between military and civil control in India and the personal contest between two arrogant, powerful men. Eventually a compromise situation was arrived at, whereby the Commander-in-Chief would have a regular Council seat with more administrative power, while a second general would have an ordinary seat and would be called a 'military supply member'. Curzon, as agreed, submitted the name of a candidate for the new post – and this was promptly vetoed by Kitchener, who went behind Curzon's back by lobbying against him in Whitehall's Army Department. The Secretary of State asked Curzon to suggest someone else. Angered by this affront, Curzon resigned.

As **Stanley Wolpert** commented:

> *Never before had a viceroy as powerful as Curzon been overruled on so relatively minor a matter, and never again would a viceroy so brilliant or imperious be appointed by Whitehall.*

Now you have read about Curzon's rule as Viceroy in India, use the information and ideas here to answer the question:

- How far would you agree with the view that Curzon made a 'colossal failure' of his job as Viceroy?

THE INDIAN CIVIL SERVICE

Joining the ICS

The Indian Civil Service was based in India and was responsible for administering the country. In doing so, the ICS became renowned for its efficiency and was the model for administrators throughout the British Empire. Young men wanting a career in the Indian Civil Service had first to pass a competitive examination and then to spend time in India working with a district officer. Leadership and all-round intelligence were prized more than academic achievement, because members of the ICS had to be able to turn their hands to anything, from tax assessment to school prize-givings; from sorting out local disputes to advising on the treatment of a rogue elephant.

Working for the ICS

When they were still young men, district officers had authority over thousands of Indians. ICS district officers developed different attitudes and different sorts of expertise, depending on the districts for which they were responsible. Men administering the Punjab, for example, became expert in agricultural matters, while those in Bengal had to deal with a rapidly rising educated, professional business class of Indian. Some, of course, were not interested in staying too long 'in the field'. Those who did so were suspected of having 'gone native', of developing too much sympathy with the plight of the Indians to the detriment of the ruling British. Ambitious young men worked for a short time as district officers and then applied for promotion to the government offices in provincial capitals. Here, some of them became overwhelmed by the sheer volume of paperwork. On the one hand, the network of railways and roads, telephone, postal and telegraphic systems built by British engineers helped the efficient administration of India. On the other hand, they meant that letters, instructions, questionnaires and directives could be sent out in their hundreds to all corners of the Indian Empire, and replies analysed and filed for future reference. Many times the system came close to grinding to a halt under the sheer weight of bureaucracy. It was systems like this that tended to stifle innovation and block radical thinking.

But the one thing nearly all British administrators had in common was their deeply held conviction that the British had a god-given right to be in India and that that right carried with it a responsibility to the Indian people.

In 1932, Sir Walter Lawrence, who joined the ICS in 1879, explained:

> *Ruling India was splendid slavery. Looking back it seems a divine drudgery, and we all felt that the work was good. We were proud of it; we were knights errant.*

Members of the ICS were well paid. This was because they were expected to be above the sort of bribery the government expected them to be offered by Indians anxious to have their particular project, village or family favoured.

Could Indian people work as administrators?

It was possible, but very difficult, for Indians to work in the Indian Civil Service. **Stanley Reed**, a British journalist in early twentieth century India, explains:

> *There was nothing on paper to stop the Indian from competing in the Civil Service examinations, but to do this he had to sit the exams in London and round off his education at a British university. He or his family had to find the ready cash, certainly not less than £1,000. The candidate had to face the risks of higher education in a foreign country and a severe test in unfamiliar surroundings. A limited number of Indians won through, and some attained high office. So serious was this handicap that in a personnel of twelve hundred in the early part of this century not more than fifty were natives.*

> (Stanley Reed, *The India I Knew*)

It wasn't until 1919 that ICS exams were held in Delhi and Rangoon, as well as in Britain.

Although, in 1900, there were few Indians in the Indian Civil Service, Indians did work with the British in other ways. Indians worked as policemen, lawyers and soldiers, for example, but there were always, at least at the beginning of the twentieth century, British officers and officials above them.

How much of India did the British govern?

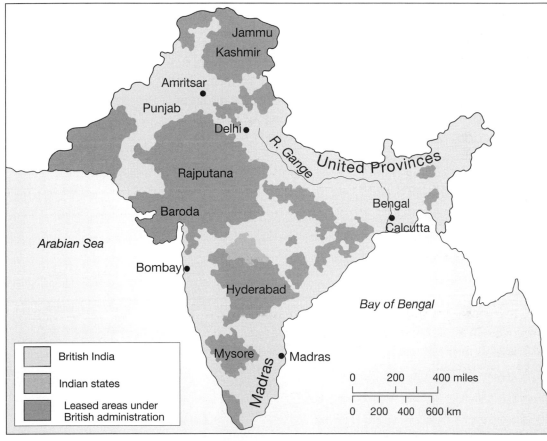

British India

Indian states

Leased areas under British administration

Areas of India that were governed directly by the British, and those that were governed indirectly, through the Indian princes c.1900

HOW WERE THE PRINCELY STATES GOVERNED?

The British provinces of India, such as Bombay, Punjab and Madras, were ruled directly by the British government through the Viceroy and the Indian Civil Service. But, as can be seen from the map above, there were vast areas of India that did not seem to be subject to the British Raj. About 35 per cent of the country, consisting of 562 separate states, was ruled by princes. Some of these states were large – about the size of Wales. Hyderabad, for example, covered 77,000 square kilometres and contained around 14 million people. Others were tiny, consisting of a few hundred people. Kathiwar was only a few square kilometres in size and had fewer than 200 inhabitants. How were these states governed?

Treaty arrangements

Rulers of the princely states had, in theory, complete authority over those whom they ruled. Practice, however, was somewhat different. They all had treaty arrangements with Britain. These treaties allowed a degree of local autonomy. Each state could keep its own laws, languages, holidays, ministers and ruler. But each state was under the 'protection' of Britain, and so, in reality, could not

KEY TERMS

Indian rulers had many different titles. These included **Maharajah** (great king) **Badshah** and **Raja** (king), and *Nawab* (governor).

The British government translated them all as 'prince' in order to avoid the implication that native rulers could be kings with status equal to that of the British monarch.

Celebrations in a princely state where a new maharajah has succeeded to the throne. The British officer is riding in state on the elephant to the maharaja's palace

instigate any action that ran counter to the interests of the British Raj. If, for example, a princely state wanted to set up an industry to manufacture railway carriages, or even the upholstery for such carriages, the Raj would not allow this. The treaties would be carefully looked over, the removal of aid and other support would be threatened, and the railways themselves would be forbidden to buy any such products. It simply would not happen.

The Resident

The four largest princely states – Hyderabad, Mysore, Jammu and Kashmir, and Baroda – were under the direct administration of the Viceroy. He was represented in these states by a Resident whom he appointed. This not only gave these particular princely states status above the others, but in effect created a 'hot line' to the seat of power in India.

The Political Officer

The remaining princely states which were deemed by Britain not to be as important as the four largest ones, had Political Officers instead of a Resident. These Political Officers were answerable to the administrators of India's provinces. Five princely states were under the authority of the Political Officer of Madras, 354 of Bombay, 26 of Bengal, 2 of Assam, 34 of Punjab, 15 of the Central Provinces and Berar, and 2 of the United Provinces.

Although the princes were treated with elaborate courtesy, they were never allowed to forget that the British did not regard them as equal allies. Believing it was their duty to guard the princes' subjects as best they could, the British, in the treaties made with the princely states, had insisted on the right to intervene and to administer a princely state if they felt it was being misgoverned. Thus, while they valued their princely allies, the British never quite believed that they ruled their subjects as well as the Raj could, if only it was given the opportunity to do so.

WAS POWER-SHARING A POSSIBILITY?

During the final years of the nineteenth century, there was a slow but steady increase within India of western-educated Indians. The British administration in India became gradually aware that they should make some sort of accommodation with these highly educated and influential Indians. The Great Rebellion had given the British a fright; it had shown the more perceptive amongst them just what could happen if the rulers became seriously out of touch with the ruled. What, many British were beginning to argue, could be more sensible than using these educated Indians to alert the Raj to potential problems and advise as to possible strategies? Furthermore, although Indians such as these could not claim to represent Indian society, they were a legitimate interest group which, the British argued, should be taken seriously.

In the immediate aftermath of the Great Rebellion, the British set up a number of consultative councils that were intended to give them 'ears to the ground'. But the British were careful not to give these councils any real power – they were, after all, to operate in an advisory capacity only. The British made sure, too, that the councillors were their nominees and, later, that they were elected on a franchise that was biased in favour of the educated and the wealthy Indian.

- The 1861 Indian Councils Act reorganised the Viceroy's Legislative Council, which advised the Viceroy and his provincial governors, and allowed for provincial legislative councils to be set up. Members of these councils, however, were chosen by government, not elected, and, as they were only permitted to discuss legislation but not enact it, their role was somewhat limited. Even so, the Secretary of State for India, Sir Charles Wood, clearly believed that this Act was of immense importance:

  'The Act is a great experiment. That everything is changing in India is obvious enough, and that the old autocratic government cannot stand unmodified is indisputable.'

- In 1883 Lord Ripon (Viceroy 1880–84) introduced a local self-government plan. Most Indian towns already had municipal corporations or councils, and some districts had local rural boards as well. Indians usually formed a majority on these bodies. From 1883, they were given extra powers to raise money for local works. This had the advantage of reducing the financial cost to the Raj and of making local bodies responsible to their electorate. Municipal corporations and rural boards would soon be voted out of power if they tried to raise and spend too much of their electorate's money. This was regarded by the Raj more as a cost cutting exercise than a move toward local self government.

  'We shall not subvert the British Empire by allowing the Bengali Baboo to discuss his own schools and drains',

  commented Sir Evelyn Baring, secretary to the Viceroy. Indeed, since the 1860s the British Raj had suffered a series of budgetary crises due, amongst other things, to the increasing cost of defending the empire. The Ripon reforms offered an ideal way of saving money.

- Two years later, the first Indian National Congress was convened (see pages 44–45) and met in Bombay. At first, it was just that   a congress, a discussion forum. It certainly was not a political party and could not, at this stage, even be described as a movement. It was not unique, either: a similar convention was held at the same time in Bombay, though they were to merge the following year. And it was not exclusively Indian: its founder was a former British Secretary for Agriculture in the Calcutta government. What does seem to have been happening at this point was that Indian opinion was beginning to be articulated in a far more formal context than ever before.

- The 1892 Indian Councils Act allowed municipalities and district boards to 'recommend' additional members to the provincial legislative councils. This was the first real opportunity for educated Indians to take part in a formal consultative process that was part of the structure of the Raj. As well as discussing legislation (allowed under the 1861 Act) councils in future could also discuss finance and ask questions of the executive, and expect them to be answered. Even so, the majority of people sitting on provincial councils were still officials of the Raj.

HOW LIMITED WAS THE RAJ?

The British Raj might seem to have been all-powerful in India, and the Indian Empire a kind of model super-state, an example to which the rest of the British Empire should aspire. But was this, in reality, the case? Just how much control did the British have in India?

- The British had an army in India and could, if necessary, call upon regiments stationed elsewhere in the Empire and in Britain. But an army was a blunt instrument when it came to crowd control and the management of demonstrations. For this, the British had to rely on the police and they were stretched very thinly indeed. Large towns like Madras had one policeman to every 2000 inhabitants and in the countryside the police were almost non-existent. So, while India was spared invasion and inter-state conflict, murders, muggings and riots were commonplace.
- There were only a few personnel available in the ICS for district administration. This meant that most of the day-to-day work had to be undertaken by low-paid Indians. Many of these Indian officials were corrupt. They took bribes, falsified records and found employment for their friends and relatives. In 1884 in the Tanjore District, for example, over 800,000 rupees that should have gone into the district revenue, ended up in the pockets of a group of Madrasi Brahmins led by the collector's chief native assistant. Thus British authority was often severely compromised by local people who were working to different agendas. Much depended on deals struck and favours that could be bought.
- The value of the support given to the British by the Indian princes was often doubtful. Several times toward the end of the nineteenth century, the British

had intervened in the internal affairs of a state to correct gross injustices and mismanagements, and in some cases deposed the sitting ruler before reforms could be instituted.

CONCLUSION

The administrative structure set up by the British in India provided an effective framework within which the power of the British Raj could be exercised. However, this was a framework only. What became known in the twentieth century as the Raj's 'steel frame' was still made predominantly of British manpower. The British were unable to rule simply by force. They were reliant on thousands of Indians, whom they kept as subordinates and whose loyalty they perceived as doubtful, to keep the wheels of administration turning. The exercise of British power depended very much on the cooperation of the Indian people.

SUMMARY QUESTIONS

1   What were the strengths of the system set up by the British to enable them to govern India?

2   Why do you think the British were unwilling to permit Indians to enter the ICS but were far more prepared to allow them a voice in provincial councils?

3   What were the weaknesses of the British Raj?

4   How could the weaknesses of the British Raj be exploited by those who wanted to overturn it?

CHAPTER 3

Change and continuity 1900–19

In the years to 1900, the British Raj had developed strategies for ensuring that it was never again caught unawares by a rising as devastating as the Great Rebellion. A major strategy was to embark on a process whereby a small number of carefully selected Indians were enabled to participate, albeit marginally, in the Raj's decision-making process. A second, no less important, strategy was to devolve some financial management to Indians to enable them to manage their own affairs at a local level. Thus the need for some sort of rapprochement with the Indian people was not really questioned by any of the British in positions of authority. The problem was to decide how much to give and when to give it.

Twice during the early twentieth century the British were forced by pressure of events to face this dilemma: between 1906 and 1909 and again between 1916 and 1919. How the imperial authorities reacted and what the impact of this was on India and Indian affairs was to have a profound impact on the direction Indian politics were to take.

This somewhat careful and almost unwilling rapprochement was running in tandem with a growing sense of national consciousness amongst the Indian people. Ironically, this sense of national consciousness was engendered by the Raj itself. All Indians who had any contact with their new rulers were immediately aware of the 'foreign' nature of these white Christian people. Although India had been invaded many times in the past, only the British invaders controlled India from a power base thousands of miles away. The influx of Christian missionaries and the continuing process of British modernisation served to intensify the sense of 'otherness', of difference among the Indians.

INDIAN NATIONALISM
In 1883, Allan Octavian Hume, a former member of the Indian Civil Service who rose to be Secretary of the

Revenue and Agriculture Department and who was an outspoken critic of the Raj, wrote an open letter to Calcutta University graduates. In it he said that

'if only 50 men can be found with sufficient power of self-sacrifice, sufficient love for and pride in their country, sufficient genuine and unselfish heartfelt patriotism to take the initiative, India can be reborn.'

Two years later, in 1885, 73 representatives from every province of British India met in Bombay at the first annual meeting of the Indian National Congress presided over by Womesh C. Bonnerjee, a barrister of the Calcutta High Court. Simultaneously, a national conference of the Indian Association, an organisation started by the Bengali politician and editor, Surendranath Banerjea, was held in Calcutta. The Bombay meeting, however, was more prestigious and more broadly based, and the following year the two were to merge. The holding of these two conferences was indicative of the need felt by the movers and shakers of Indian opinion for a more formal forum in which to discuss, shape and direct Indian national sentiment.

Who attended the first meeting of the Indian National Congress?

Most of the delegates at the Congress were high-caste Hindus, all of whom spoke English and most of whom were lawyers, although there was a smattering of teachers, journalists and businessmen among them, along with some wealthy landowners and merchants. The delegates were not exclusively Indian. Allan Hume, for example, who had been instrumental in calling the Congress in the first place – and who was a close friend of the Liberal politician Lord Ripon (Viceroy 1880–84) – attended and played a key advisory role. It is important to emphasise that in these early days Congress was simply a forum for discussion. It was not a political party and could not even, in any sense, be called a movement. Later, however it was to become the organisational vehicle for India's first great nationalist movement.

Hindu or Muslim?

Congress was, at the start, dominated by Hindus, most of whom were high-caste. Although a substantial number of

Parsis and Jains attended, there were, significantly, only two Muslims. This situation had changed by the time of the third annual meeting of Congress, held in Madras, where 83 of the 600 delegates were Muslim. However, this domination of Congress by Hindus was to continue and India's largest minority community never felt easy under the umbrella of Congress. This led them to turn to and create alternative political organisations that were themselves to pursue a different sort of nationalist agenda.

What did the first meeting of Congress want?

The delegates met for three days and everyone proclaimed their loyalty to the British crown and, by extension, to the Raj. However, all the people who spoke expressed some level of dissatisfaction with the ways in which the Raj was governing India. Delegates wanted:

- the basis of the government of India to be widened so that the 'people should have their proper and legitimate share in it'
- the opening of the Indian Civil Service to Indians
- opportunities for Indians to serve on various government councils
- more of India's wealth to be spent on internal improvements and less on the military
- the abolition of the Secretary of State's council in Whitehall, viewing it as a waste of India's resources and a block to radical progress within India.

Initially, these resolutions were framed within the spirit of cooperation with the Raj, but, as you will see later, they formed the platform from which more radical demands were made, culminating in the demand for independence.

Was Congress the only way Indians were making their views heard?

Something as organised as Congress doesn't come out of nowhere. All kinds of threads, all kinds of different initiatives led to the 1885 meeting. For example:

- In 1870, the Brahmin Mahadev Govind Ranade founded the 'Sarvajanik Sabha' (All People's Association) in Poona. Its aim was to help all Indians realise their potential by making full and effective use of the existing political institutions. Although prevented by his position on the Indian bench from formally joining the Indian National Congress, he founded India's National Social Conference in 1887 which considered social issues, particularly the plight of Hindu widows.

- **Gopal Krishna Gokhale** (see Key Person box) was a follower of Ranade who developed the idea of nationalism by insisting on the need for Indians to reform their own social and religious ideas, and resolve their own internal conflicts, before they could begin to consider anything as radical as political independence.
- In 1879, a petty clerk in the government's Military Accounts Department, Vasudeo Balwant Phadke, suddenly named himself 'Minister to Shivaji II' and rode off into the hills of Maharashtra to raise an army against the Crown. This was not, perhaps, as crazy as it may sound. Shivaji (1627–80) was the founder of the Maratha kingdom. Inspired by the heroes of Hindu mythologies, he considered it his mission to liberate India from the Islamic Mughals. Phadke was following this example and, in his view, living out Hindu mythology and history. It took the British four years to catch him!
- Another nationalist, Vihnu Hari Chiplunkar, was so inspired by Phadke that he, too, left his government post. Instead of taking to the hills, he opened a private school in Poona. Chiplunkar's poetry and political essays inspired many young people, including Bal Gangadhar Tilak (see page 48)

By the beginning of the twentieth century, Indian nationalism was well established in a far more formal setting than ever before. It did not simply have a voice, it had the organisational basis from which to grow and develop as a political force.

THE MORLEY–MINTO REFORMS 1909

In 1909, **John Morley** (see page 49), the Secretary of State for India, and Lord Minto, the Viceroy, introduced a whole raft of reforms.

Why were reforms necessary?

- The backlash against Lord Curzon's partition of Bengal (see pages 33–34) had spread far beyond that province. When Minto arrived in India to take over as Viceroy from Lord Curzon, agitation against partition was at its height. Minto was himself threatened with assassination.

- Towards the end of 1906, the Lieutenant-Govenor of the Punjab, Denzil Ibbetson, faced such unrest that he feared an uprising similar to the Great Rebellion 50 years earlier. Beginning as a protest against proposals for higher charges and stricter regulations for settlers in areas irrigated by government-funded waterways, the situation escalated at such a rate that Ibbetson feared a conspiracy. Riots and murders were commonplace and there were rumours that the Punjabi army was on the point of mutiny. However, the whole affair turned out to be something of a damp squib.

Minto suspected a conspiracy, Morley, the Secretary of State for India, did not. An inquiry into the loyalty of the Punjabi soldiers revealed that they had been considerably swayed by agitators, who had urged them to strike in order to gain redress of grievances such as pay and promotion prospects. At this critical point, Ibbetson left India for medical treatment in England. The potential threat to the loyalty of the whole Punjabi army, and the devastating consequences this would have on the Raj, convinced Minto that the proposed charges and regulations should be withdrawn, and they were. The Punjabis went wild with delight and made their continuing loyalty to the Crown abundantly clear.

- The Indian National Congress was growing increasingly concerned about the extremists in its midst and by the power struggle that was going on within Congress between the extremists and the moderates. John Morley, in particular, was influenced by Gopal Krishna Gokhale, the highly educated, moderate Indian who visited England many times and with whom Morley had many frank discussions about the difficulties faced by Indians in positions of influence in maintaining a moderate stance.

John Morley, back in England, and Lord Minto, on the spot in India, together became convinced that more concessions had to be made to the Indian people. Indians had to be drawn in still further to the process of government. It had become clear that politically active Indians could, in certain circumstances, sway the masses behind them. They recognised that loyalty to the British Raj had to be both encouraged and rewarded.

What was the significance of the Simla Deputation?

Agitation by the Indian National Congress against the partition of Bengal was mainly a protest against the 'divide and rule' policy that Viceroy Curzon and the governor of Bengal were attempting to carry out. Many Muslims, however, believed that the agitation showed that they would not be fairly treated by any organisation with a Hindu majority. To safeguard their interests, Muslim leaders drew up a plan for separate electorates and presented it to the Viceroy, Lord Minto, at Simla in 1906.

The Simla Deputation consisted of some 70 delegates representing all shades of Muslim opinion. The deputation stressed that the Muslim community should not be judged by its numerical strength alone but by its political importance and the service it had rendered to the Empire. The deputation further pointed out that western ideas of democracy were not appropriate for India and stressed the need for care when introducing or extending the electoral system in whatever sphere – local or national.

Minto replied by assuring the Simla Deputation that their political rights and interests as a community would be safeguarded in any administrative reorganisation in which he was involved. This assurance was to have long-term significance as the Raj struggled to give Indians a greater say in their own affairs.

What were the reforms proposed by Morley and Minto?

John Morley seems to have been the driving force behind the reforms that were finally agreed. It was Lord Minto who proposed a series of moderate reforms that he said would 'satisfy the legitimate aspirations of all but the most advanced Indians' and John Morley who came back with much more radical proposals. Minto, for example, envisaged a modest increase in the number of Indians nominated by the Raj to serve on the various councils, while Morley proposed a larger number of Indian representatives and wanted them to be elected. Morley was determined to reduce the number of officials (invariably white and invariably British) serving on provincial councils and on the Viceroy's executive council.

The reforms that were finally agreed between John Morley and Lord Minto were announced in November 1908 and enshrined in the Indian Councils Act of 1909.

- Sixty Indian representatives were to be elected to serve on the Viceroy's executive council; 27 of these were to be elected from territorial constituencies and special-interest groups. However, officials remained in the majority.
- The provincial councils were to be enlarged sufficiently to create non-official majorities.
- Separate electorates were provided for Muslims and Hindus in order to allow the minority Muslims to have a voice in the various councils.

Additionally, John Morley appointed two Indians to his London-based group of advisers. Minto, responding to Morley's urging to act in a similar way, appointed Satyendra Sinha, the Advocate-General of Bengal, to be his Law member. However, Minto and his officials in Calcutta, although believing the reforms to be essential, thought of them as a defensive action. Morley, on the other hand, regarded them as a significant step towards colonial self-government.

What were the effects of the Morley–Minto reforms?

By far the most important effect of the Morley–Minto reforms was that from 1909 onwards, Indians were involved in policy making both in India and, because of John Morley's nominations, in Britain too. Their voice, at this stage, may not have been loud, but it was a voice that was legally entitled to be heard.

However, there were those for whom the reforms were either too much or too little.

The 'extremists'

The right to vote was restricted to the rich and privileged. Indian vested interests were protected because seats were reserved for landowners and members of chambers of commerce. These were exactly the sort of moderate men who could be expected to support the Raj. Thousands of politically-minded Indians expected more; the extremists were isolated and regarded the reforms as nothing more than cynical window-dressing on the part of the Raj. They continued their fight for full Indian self-government, and terrorism in all its forms continued.

Administrators

Many British administrators were disappointed and disheartened by the changes, which diluted their power. They were no longer in the majority on provincial councils and had to contend with a substantial Indian minority on the Viceroy's executive council. Indeed, Sir

The 1911 Delhi durbar, held to celebrate the coronation of King George V. At the same time, the capital of India was moved from Calcutta to Delhi, the power base of the old Mughal Empire.

Bampfylde Fuller, the governor (for a brief time) of partitioned east Bengal described the reforms as 'conciliatory sugar plums'. It was British administrators like these who genuinely believed that they governed India in the best interests of the Indians. They believed that, divided by faction, caste, and religion, Indian people could not be expected to govern India impartially. Dispassionate judgement, they maintained, was beyond the mentality of the Indians.

The ICS had, for years, maintained that they spoke for the vast mass of Indian people. They couldn't maintain this stance any longer and so believed their influence had been diminished. They feared for their future.

Congress

Congress, dominated by Hindus, while generally supporting the reforms, bitterly regretted that electoral procedures were designed to achieve a balance of minority interests. Muslim interests were protected by creating a separate electorate for them and by imposing lower property and educational qualifications for Muslim voters than for Hindus. Congress would have had it otherwise.

The iron hand in the velvet glove?

Over one hundred years of all-white, colonial rule had ended. Colonial rule, on the other hand, most definitely had not. The Morley–Minto reforms were announced in November 1908, the fiftieth anniversary of the British takeover of the administration of India from the East India Company. The decision to reunite Bengal was proclaimed at King George V's coronation **durbar** in December 1911. These were not coincidences. They were public reminders that the future of India was still determined by the British Crown and the British Parliament.

WHAT WAS THE IMPACT ON INDIA OF THE FIRST WORLD WAR (1914–18)?

Involvement in the war

The outbreak of war in Europe was met with instant loyalty and declarations of support across all sections of Indian society. Offers of support poured in from the

KEY EVENT

Durbar In Mughal India, durbars were ceremonial gatherings to receive visitors in audience, conduct official business and confer honours.

The British Raj adopted the idea and held great ceremonial events which they called durbars. Lord Lytton held a durbar, for example, when Queen Victoria was proclaimed Empress of India in 1876. The great Delhi durbars of 1903 and 1911 were staged to celebrate the coronations of the British kings Edward VII and George V. These were fantastic ceremonial displays, involving hundreds of maharajas, and bejewelled elephants, music and dancing.

The Muslim League The
All-India Muslim League
was founded at the annual
Muhammadan Educational
Conference held in Dhaka
in December 1906. About
3000 delegates attended
and supported Nawab Salim
Ullah Khan's proposal that a
political party be established
to look after the interests
of Muslims: the All-India
Muslim League.

princely states, from Congress and from the **Muslim League**. Even Tilak, leader of the extremist faction in Congress, declared 'our sense of loyalty is inherent and unswerving'. Twenty-seven of the largest princely states immediately put their Imperial Service Troops at the Viceroy's disposal. A hospital ship, The *Loyalty*, was commissioned, fully fitted and provisioned by the princes. Recruitment exceeded all expectations, and Indian troops were soon sailing for Flanders, Gallipoli and Mesopotamia, serving overseas as combatants and support staff, dwarfing all other Imperial contributions to the war effort. By November 1918, some 827,000 Indians had enlisted as combatants, in addition to those already serving in 1914. It seems from official figures that around 64,449 Indian soldiers died in the war.

The Western Front

In August and September 1914, as German troops swept through Belgium into France, decimating the British Expeditionary Force, fresh, new troops were desperately needed. The Indian Army, with 161,000 trained soldiers, seemed the obvious choice. The first Indian Expeditionary Force, made up of 16,000 British and 28,500 Indian troops of the Lahore and Meerut divisions and the Secunderabad Cavalry brigade, embarked from Karachi on 24 August 1914, reaching Marseilles on 26 September. They got to the Western Front just in time for the first Battle of Ypres. There, their losses were heavy: the average Indian battalion had 764 fighting men and by early November the 47th Sikhs, for example, were down to 385 fit soldiers. In early 1915, the Indian regiments were rested, but were soon back in the trenches. They provided half the Allied fighting force at Neuve Chapelle, and the Lahore division was thrown into the counter-attack at the second Battle of Ypres in April 1915.

In December 1915, the two infantry divisions were withdrawn from France and sent to the Middle East. Some historians argue that this was because of their low morale and War Office fears that the Indians could not survive another winter on the Western Front. On the other hand, it made perfect sense to concentrate the Indian Army in the Middle East, where it was easier to

HEINEMANN ADVANCED HISTORY

send supplies and reinforcements from India. Two Indian cavalry divisions remained on the Western Front until March 1918, when they were transferred to Palestine to take part in operations against the Turks.

The problem of religion

Religion only became a problem after Turkey entered the war because, in the eyes of Muslims, the British Empire was now at war with a Muslim power. Muslims in the Indian Army faced a huge dilemma. Most Muslim soldiers agreed that the war was still lawful, although there were desertions from Muslim units on the Western Front and elsewhere. There were also at least three mutinies of Muslim troops, usually when they thought they were going to be sent to fight against Turks.

Attitudes to fighting

For most Indian soldiers, going to war was part of their well-established ancestral tradition of obligation to whomsoever was their emperor. Interestingly, few claimed to be fighting for India. Most cited the King or the Empire as legitimate causes for which they were fighting. In the case of the 1914–18 war, their king emperor was George V and so they loyally enlisted under his colours. This attitude was reflected in their letters home from the Front.

- Havildar Singh wrote from the western front in September 1915: 'If I die I go to Paradise. It is a fine thing to die in battle. We must honour him who feeds us. Our dear government's rule is very good and gracious.'
- Pirhan Dyal, also serving in France, wrote: 'We must be true to our salt and he who is faithful will go to paradise.'
- A Jat non-commissioned officer, recovering from his wounds, wrote home: 'Who remembers a man who dies in his bed? But it is our duty as Khastris to kill the enemy and then a man becomes a hero.'
- The sister of three brothers stationed in Egypt wrote: 'War is the task of young men, to sport with death upon the field of battle, to be as a tiger and to draw the sword of honour and daring.'

Compromising internal control?

Thousands upon thousands of Indians left India to fight in the Imperial cause. Thousands of British troops stationed in India left too, withdrawn to support Allied troops in France and Mesopotamia. Along with them went many ICS men and expatriate civilians, who volunteered to fight in the armed forces. Indeed, in 1914 Viceroy Hardinge warned of 'the risks involved in denuding India of troops' and admitted that 'there is no disguising the fact that our position in India is a bit of a gamble at the present time'. By March 1915 there was not a single regular British battalion left in India. Any sort of uprising in this situation would be very difficult to contain.

Great expectations?

The presence of so many Indian soldiers fighting alongside British and white colonial battalions not only increased the self-esteem of the Indians, but also strengthened the arguments of Indian politicians that Indians should be given a greater say in Indian affairs. The Allies, in rallying support for their cause, frequently referred to the war as one being fought to defend the rights of nations and the sanctity of treaties. They spoke, too, of the importance of democracy and of **self-determination**. As the Indians listened and assimilated these values, they began to apply them to their own situation back in India.

Indeed, as early as 1914 a little-known lawyer, **Mohandas Gandhi**, urged Indians to give

> *'such humble assistance as we may be considered capable of performing, as an earnest declaration of our desire to share the responsibilities of membership of a great Empire just as we would share its privileges.'*

Here, in Gandhi's statement, the implications seem clear. If India took its share of responsibilities in time of war, then it would have shown itself worthy of self-government. Was this the price Britain would have to pay for Indian support throughout the First World War?

KEY CONCEPT

Self-determination The right of all nations to determine their own future.

What was the economic impact of the First World War?

Economics and politics frequently go hand-in-hand. A prosperous economy tends to make individuals and whole nations more self-confident and more inclined to pursue their objectives in national and international contexts. Similarly, economic problems involving unemployment, crop failures and the like can make people turn on those who govern them and demand change. The outcomes look very similar although the causes are different. Such was the case with India.

Winners and losers

India had poured men and materials into the war effort and in doing so had become a crucial source of supply for the Allied cause. By the end of December 1919, some 1.5 million Indians had been recruited into combatant and non-combatant roles, and nearly all of them had been sent overseas along with 184,350 animals.

By the end of the First World War, Indian revenues had contributed over £146m to the Allied war effort. About half of this amount was made up of war loans, which in 1917 raised £35.5m and in 1918 a further £38m. Military expenditure had risen dramatically, too, and revenue demands here were raised by 16 per cent in 1916–17, 14 per cent in 1917–18 and 10 per cent in 1918–19. Thus most ordinary people felt the effects of the war through increased taxation.

People were bothered, too, by shortages of fuel and by rising prices. During the war prices of food grains rose by 93 per cent, of Indian made goods by 60 per cent and imported goods by 190 per cent. These rises were brought about by the disruption of war to normal trading patterns, exchange rate problems and the demands of the military. The government tried to control prices, but was too often frustrated by profiteers and speculators. The situation was exacerbated by the failure of the monsoons to arrive in 1918–19 and consequent grain shortages and famine. Life for many was hard, just as it was on the home front in western European countries. Yet the war did benefit some, and not just the speculators and profiteers. Indian manufacturing industries, particularly cotton, iron and steel, sugar, engineering and chemicals, expanded in order to replace goods normally imported. Shareholders saw their dividends rocket. In Bombay, dividends from cloth mills jumped from 6 per cent in 1914 to over 30 per cent in 1917. In Ahmedabad, the cotton manufacturing centre of India, one mill-owner reported a trebling of profits.

It was against this background that the Viceroy had to juggle the demands of London for India's resources and the concerns of his district officers at localised distress and disturbances as they watched prices spiralling out of control. In some areas groups of local government officials went on strike and there was serious concern in some provincial governments that local support for the Raj was crumbling. By 1918 the Viceroy's office in Delhi was receiving regular reports from provincial legislatures of food riots, petty violence and looting. It was fortunate for British rule in India that these outbreaks were sporadic and never coalesced into a general campaign against increased taxation. If it had done, the withdrawal of so many troops to Europe and the departure of hundreds of ICS men and expatriate civilians, would have made the domestic Indian situation very tricky, to say the least. Indeed, as early as 1914 Viceroy Hardinge had warned about 'the risks involved in denuding India of troops: there is no disguising the fact that our position in India is a bit of a gamble at the present time'.

It was hardly surprising that the economic effects of war very rapidly had political repercussions.

What were the political effects of the First World War?

The political problems posed by the war were infinitely more complicated than attempting to deal with local protests against intolerable localised conditions. Issues were created that could only be dealt with in India because they focused on the nature of Britain's relationship with India and the Indian people. Broad national shifts in the political spectrum had been created that were to present serious challenges to the Raj.

- Indian soldiers had fought alongside white British and colonial forces, strengthening their self-esteem.
- Indian political arguments that the war should be a turning point in Indian–Raj relationships were also strengthened as a consequence.
- Indians were beginning to apply to their own situation the concepts of democracy and freedom for which their European and, later, US allies said they were fighting.

Congress and the Muslim League

As early as 1915, Congress was speaking openly about self-government and about the changes in attitude that the war was bringing. This is part of a speech made in that year by the Congress President, Surendranath Banerjea:

> *The idea of re-adjustment is in the air, not only here in India but all the world over. The heart of the Empire is set upon it. What is this war for? Why are these enormous sufferings endured? Because it is a war of re-adjustment, a war that will set right the claims of minor nationalities... They are talking about what will happen after the war in Canada, in Australia; they are talking about it from the floor of the House of Commons and in the gatherings of public men and ministers of the state. May we not also talk about it a little from our standpoint?*

By 1916, the political situation in India had hardened, largely because the Muslim League and Congress had buried their differences. How had this happened? The annulment of the partition of Bengal had alarmed the Muslim League. Believing this meant that the British would no longer regard them as a separate community deserving of separate electoral treatment, they had tried to find some sort of accommodation with the Hindus. In this they had been successful, helped in no small part by the efforts of the Englishwoman **Annie Besant** and her All-India Home Rule League, the Muslim leader Muhammad Ali Jinnah and the Hindu extremist, Tilak.

The Lucknow Pact of 1916 was an agreement between Congress and the Muslim League whereby it was agreed that Muslims would have a fixed proportion of seats in an Indian parliament and extra seats in areas where they

Annie Besant (1847–1933) Born in London to Irish parents, Annie Besant was a prominent social reformer in England and was Vice-President of the National Secular Society and a freethinker. She formed a close friendship with Charles Bradlaugh with whom she co-edited *The National Reformer*, and with whom in 1875 she was prosecuted for spreading information about birth control. She became a socialist, joined the Fabian Society and worked to publicise trade union issues, being instrumental in organising the Bryant and May's match-girls' strike.

In 1889 Annie was converted to theosophy, seeing in it a link between socialism and spirituality. She visited India in 1893, where the headquarters of the Theosophical Society were located, and, deciding it was her true home, settled there for the rest of her life.

Annie learned Sanskrit, studied the Hindu scriptures and was determined to raise Hindu self-esteem in the face of the imperialism of the British Raj. She founded the Central Hindu College in 1898 and a network of schools throughout India administered by the Theosophical Society. After 1913 Annie turned her attention to Indian independence and in 1917 was appointed President of Congress. Gradually, however, she lost nationalist support and was eclipsed by the campaigns of Gandhi.

were in a minority. Thus the Muslims believed they had been given assurances by the Hindus that were similar to those obtained earlier from the British government, and felt themselves able to work with the Hindu-dominated Congress. In a similar way, the deaths of the moderates Gopal Gokhale and Pherozeshah Mehta enabled Congress to find a formula whereby the extremist Bal Tilak could re-enter Congress. It was hardly surprising that one of the first resolutions passed in 1916 by the newly united Congress was to urge the British to 'issue a proclamation stating it is the aim and intention of British policy to confer self-government on India at an early date'.

The Imperial Legislative Council

The attitude of Congress was reflected in the Viceroy's Imperial Legislative Council. The following year, in 1917, Madan Mohan Malaviya (Congress President 1909 and 1918, and member of the Imperial Legislative Council 1910–20) spoke about the differences the war had made:

> *The question of reform is a much larger one now than it was before the war. As Mr Lloyd George {the British Prime Minister} said the other day, the war has changed us very much. It has changed the angle of vision in India as well as in England … All will have to recognise that the reforms after the war will have to be such as will meet the requirements of India today and of tomorrow, such as will satisfy the aspirations of her people to take their legitimate part in the administration of their own country.*

Home Rule Leagues

The claims made by Congress and the Imperial Legislative Council were backed by two totally new and innovative organisations that were set up in 1916: the Home Rule Leagues. Their aim was to stimulate public opinion and organise public pressure for Home Rule for India. One was started by Bal Tilak and operated mainly in western India; the other was founded by Annie Besant and spread throughout the rest of the country. Both organisations used newspapers, rallies, vernacular pamphlets, preachers and songs in an attempt to reach the masses who hitherto had been uninterested in the doings of Congress, the Muslim League and the Imperial

Legislative Council. It worked. After one year, over 60,000 Indians had joined the Home Rule Leagues. The conventional assemblies were alarmed by the outspoken demands of these Leagues, the British Raj even more so: the two leaders were banned from several provinces, students were forbidden to attend their meetings and Annie Besant was interned in June 1917.

How would the British government react to these demands for self-government?

EDWIN MONTAGU, LORD CHELMSFORD AND THE GOVERNMENT OF INDIA ACT 1919

The British government faced a huge dilemma. They could not ignore the enormous sacrifices made by the Indian people and the steadfast loyalty they had shown to the British Crown. They were aware that the Indian people and their politicians were looking for a reward for this loyalty. They could not ignore, either, their own belief in the rights of people to democracy and self-determination. On the other hand, they faced the spectacle of the overthrow of Tsardom in Russia, seen by many Indian politicians as a sign that a new day was dawning, and to the British establishment as a sign that anarchy was just around the corner.

What was the Montagu Declaration?

July 1917 saw Edwin Montagu as Secretary of State at the India Office. A passionate Liberal, who had worked under John Morley at the India Office before the war, Montagu was clear that a straightforward statement of British policy toward India was essential. In association with Lord Chelmsford, the Viceroy, the Montagu Declaration was formulated and agreed by the British government:

> *The policy of His Majesty's Government, with which the Government of India are in complete accord, is that of the increasing association of Indians in every branch of the administration and the gradual development of self-governing institutions with a view to the progressive realisation of responsible government in India as part of the British Empire.*

Britain was now implicitly committed to allowing Indians to govern themselves, but within the context of the British Empire. Although no timescale was given, the Declaration ended by saying that Montagu would visit India to 'consider with the Viceroy the views of local governments, and to receive with him the suggestions of representative bodies and others'.

Montagu's travels

Edwin Montagu travelled extensively in India between November 1917 and May 1918, listening to all kinds of opinion from all sorts of different people. A keen ornithologist and game hunter, he found much to amaze and delight him in the activities arranged for him by the Indian princes. However, he found little to amaze and delight him in what he saw as the 'dead hand' of British administration. Very little, he believed, had changed since the days of Curzon (see pages 31–35) and slow and complex bureaucracy could, even after Curzon's administrative reforms, stifle radical ideas and reform. He was very much afraid the Viceroy would succumb to the reactionaries amongst his administration, and was particularly critical of a Colonel O'Dwyer who was adamantly opposed to any more Indian participation in government.

The Montagu–Chelmsford Report and the Government of India Act 1919

The proposals decided upon by Secretary of State Montagu and Viceroy Chelmsford were published in July 1918 and became law as the Government of India Act in December 1919.

- The Viceroy was to be advised by a Council of six civilians, three of whom had to be Indians, and the Commander-in-Chief of the British Army in India.
- The Viceroy could enforce laws even if the legislative councils rejected them, and he could choose his own officials.
- The provincial and central legislative councils were enlarged.
- The provincial councils were given control over Indian education, agriculture, health, local self-government and public works.

- The British retained control of military matters, foreign affairs, currency, communications and criminal law.
- The franchise was extended, although it was still linked to the amount and type of tax men paid. After 1919, about 10 per cent of the adult male population was enfranchised. All former soldiers were automatically given the vote.
- Provincial legislatures could give the vote to women if they wished to, and some did. Even so, the number of women voters was less than 1 per cent of the provincial adult female population.
- There were 'reserved' seats in all provincial legislatures for different religious groups (Sikhs, Muslims, Indian Christians, for example) and special interest groups like landowners and university graduates.

This system was called 'dyarchy' because it divided power in the provinces (albeit unequally) between the Indians and the British.

How did people react to the Government of India Act?

In many ways the dyarchy system was an extension of the Morley–Minto reforms ten years earlier. Like them, it tried to enlist the cooperation of India's educated middle class in governing India, but it took the Morley–Minto reforms further by shifting more and more decision-making from the centre to the provinces, and by involving more Indians in the governing of their own country. There were, however, problems:

- Montagu saw the Act as a welcome further step towards Indian self-government, and so did his horrified critics.
- In the House of Commons, India became a contentious issue. On the right, MPs were convinced the government was losing its nerve and would soon lose India; on the left, there were protests that the reforms hadn't gone far enough.
- The ICS felt its strength and influence were slipping away.
- Many Indians welcomed the Act, even though it didn't offer immediate self-government.
- Many people, British and Indian, hated the idea of 'reserved seats' with specific electorates, considering

them divisive and anti-democratic. Indeed, Montagu and Chelmsford themselves disliked the idea but felt themselves bound to respect the Lucknow Pact.

- Those Indians hoping for Home Rule were bitterly disappointed. As details of the reforms became known, unrest and violence increased, especially in the Punjab.
- The Indian National Congress rejected the Montagu–Chelmsford reforms and boycotted the first elections held under the 1919 Act.

The situation in India was exacerbated by the recession that set in when the war ended. There were lay-offs and unemployment as the demand for war materials, particularly textiles, collapsed. Added to this, the Spanish flu epidemic that hit Europe affected India, too, killing more than 13 million people. And in India the situation was worsened by the failure of the monsoon to deliver and the consequent crop failure and regional famine. Add to this the British government's very real fear of Bolshevism taking hold in post-war India (the Russian revolutions of 1917 had established a Bolshevik regime there) and it is understandable that an unstable situation was created in the sub-continent, leading to further unrest, disturbances and riots.

The British Raj responded in the only way it knew how – by repression to be enforced by the Rowlatt Acts.

WHAT WERE THE EFFECTS OF THE ROWLATT ACTS?

In a word: disastrous!

What did the Rowlatt commission propose?

As early as 1917 the Indian government, afraid that the situation was slipping away from them, appointed a Mr S. A. T. Rowlatt (a Scottish judge) to 'investigate revolutionary conspiracies'. The Rowlatt Commission reported in July 1918. It isolated Bengal, Bombay and Punjab as centres of revolutionary activity and recommended that the old wartime controls should be used there to contain the situation. These included imprisonment without trial, trial by judges sitting without a jury, censorship and house arrest of suspects. These proposals were incorporated into the Rowlatt Acts, passed in March 1919, and sanctioned by Montagu with extreme reluctance. He told the Viceroy that they were 'extremely repugnant' although he conceded he appreciated the need to stamp out rebellion and riot. However, Viceroy Chelmsford went ahead and the measure was pushed through the Imperial Legislative Council in the face of opposition from every single Indian member.

What damage did the Acts do?

In reality, the new powers were found to be unnecessary and were soon repealed. But the damage had been done. All Indian members of the Imperial Legislative Council were opposed to the Rowlatt Acts; the impression was created – loud and clear – that the promises made by the Montagu–Chelmsford reforms were meaningless. In the end, when the chips were down, it seemed that the British government was prepared to use force to crush Indian opposition. The Acts suggested, furthermore, that the British had no intention of relaxing their grip on India. Thus the Rowlatt Acts alienated a wide range of public opinion in India and came close to wrecking the 1919 Government of India Act.

CONCLUSION

The period 1900–19 was marked by both change and continuity. The British made concessions to Indian opinion in that they invited Indian participation in the decision-making process. Yet this can be seen as a way of strengthening the Raj and their control within India. For Indians, the period saw a growing awareness of their desire for self-government, heightened by their experience of the First World War. While many were satisfied with the concessions made by the British, there was a steady growth of opinion that Indians should be in complete control of their own affairs.

SUMMARY QUESTIONS

1 How effective were the Morley–Minto reforms?
2 To what extent can the First World War be seen as a watershed in Indian politics and opinions?
3 What was the significance of the Government of India Act 1919?
4 What elements of change and of continuity can be seen in the actions of the British Raj 1900–19?

CHAPTER 4

Flashpoint Amritsar!

Opposition to the Rowlatt Acts flared up throughout India, but nowhere more fiercely than in the Punjab, and nowhere more frighteningly than in the town of Amritsar, the administrative capital.

CASE STUDY: THE AMRITSAR MASSACRE – TENSIONS REVEALED?

Rioting begins

Two leading nationalists, Dr Saifuddin Kitchlew, a young Cambridge-educated barrister, and Dr Satya Pal, a medical doctor, organised a series of **hartals** (workplace lockouts, non-attendance at offices and schools and shutting up of shops) on 30 March and 6 April as a protest against the Rowlatt Acts. There was no serious unrest as a result, and the days were marked by an impressive display of Hindu–Muslim solidarity. But the authorities decided to arrest the two men and then trouble broke out on a large scale. Rioting began on 10 April, originally in support of the two detained men but quickly turned into a general anti-European attack. Banks were stormed, buildings fired and three Europeans killed. A mission doctor, Marcia Sherwood, was brutally beaten by Indian youths and only saved from death by Hindus who found her and treated her. By 11 April, over 100 terrified and exhausted European women and children had taken refuge in the Gobindgarh fort, trying to find a place of safety in a city where the British had lost control to the mob.

The British reaction

The governor of the Punjab, **Michael O'Dwyer** was convinced that the riots were part of a carefully planned uprising which would lure Indian soldiers into a mutiny. So his reaction to the situation in Amritsar was to treat it as the first stage in a general insurrection aimed at overthrowing the Raj. He ordered Brigadier General **Rex Dyer**, a tough career soldier who had been born in India and who commanded the 45th Brigade based at

Michael O'Dwyer (1864–1940) The sixth child in a large Irish family, Michael O'Dwyer passed the examinations for the Indian Civil Service and went out to India in 1885.

His first posting was to Shahpur in the Punjab, where he undertook land settlement work and was made director of land records and agriculture. He was selected by Viceroy Curzon to help sort out the new North-West Frontier Province and its separation from Punjab. He moved up through the ICS, and finally became Lieutenant Governor of the Punjab in 1912.

During his time as Governor, (1912–19) he gained a reputation for firmness and some regarded him as little less than a dictator. During his time as Governor of the Punjab the Amritsar massacre occurred. Some Indian historians believe that the massacre was planned beforehand by O'Dwyer and top British bureaucrats, but there is, as yet, little hard evidence to support this theory.

O'Dwyer was assassinated on 13 March 1940 in London by Udham Singh, a Punjabi, in revenge for the deaths during the Amritsar Massacre.

Jalandhar, to go with his men to Amritsar and sort the situation out. As Dyer left, he said to his son:

> 'Mussulmans and Hindus are united. I have been expecting this, there is a very big show coming.'

Ironically, it was Dyer himself who turned the situation into a 'big show'.

Dyer arrives at Amritsar

Dyer had under his command about 1000 troops, roughly one-third of whom were British, and two armoured cars equipped with machine guns. They stationed themselves in the Ram Bagh, a parkland area laid out as gardens, with running water and plenty of space for the men to pitch their tents. On 12th April, Dyer led 400 troops and the armoured cars through the streets of Amritsar. This was intended as a show of force, but one that didn't really work. The Indians lining the streets jeered at the troops and shouted threatening slogans such as *'The British Raj is at an end'*. Back in the Ram Bagh, Dyer was told of similar disturbances in the Punjab cities of Lahore and Kasur. He became even more convinced that a general uprising was imminent.

The following day, 13 April, was Baisakhi Day. It marked the beginning of one of the most important religious festivals in the Punjab, which lasted for several days. Thousands of pilgrims began flocking into Amritsar to worship in the Golden Temple; still more thousands came for the horse and cattle fairs that were part of the festivities. Hundreds of these people and their families converged on the Jallianwala Bagh, a large open space of about eight acres of beaten earth. They intended staying there for the duration of the festival, talking and resting and meeting with the residents of Amritsar. Arrangements were also made for a political meeting to be held in part of the Jallianwala Bagh so that people could voice their opinions and make their feelings felt about the Rowlatt Acts.

It was at 10.30 am on 13 April that Dyer and a detachment of troops re-entered Amritsar. At various

KEY PERSON

Reginald 'Rex' Edward Harry Dyer (1864–1927)
Reginald Dyer was born in Murree (then in India, now in Pakistan), grew up in Simla and attended the British school there. He joined the army as an officer in 1885 and served in riot control duties in Belfast (1886) and the Third Burma War (1886–7) He then transferred to the Indian Army, where he commanded the 25th Punjabis in India and Hong Kong.

He showed such bravery during the First World War that he was mentioned in dispatches and was made a Companion of the Bath. After the Amritsar Massacre he was again mentioned in dispatches for his bravery in the Anglo-Afghan war.

It was, however, for his conduct during the Amritsar Massacre that he will be remembered. Heavily censured by both the Hunter Commission and Congress, he was relieved of his post and recalled to England. Parliament debated his case twice, with the Lords supporting him and the Commons censuring him.

Dyer resigned his commission in 1920 and died of natural causes seven years later.

points in the city, accompanied by drumbeats to catch the crowd's attention, a proclamation was read out:

No person residing in Amritsar City is permitted to leave his house after 8.00 pm. Any persons found in the streets after 8.00 pm are liable to be shot.

No procession of any kind is permitted to parade the streets in the city or any part of the city or outside of it at any time. Any such processions or gatherings of four men will be looked upon and treated as an unlawful assembly and dispersed by force of arms if necessary.

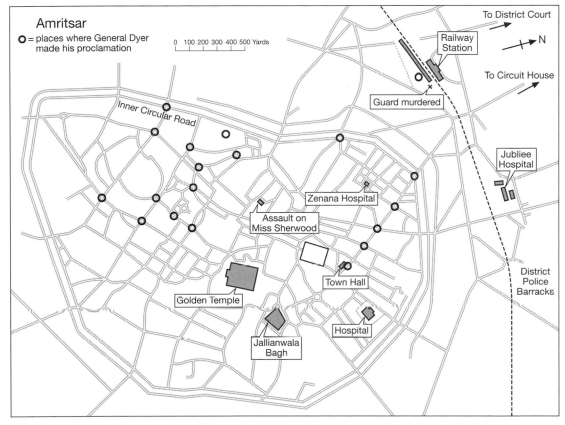

A map of Amritsar showing where General Dyer stopped to read out the proclamations

Questions

1   Do you think that making the proclamations was the right way to bring calm to Amritsar?

2   Are you surprised that no proclamations were made anywhere near to the Jallianwala Bagh?

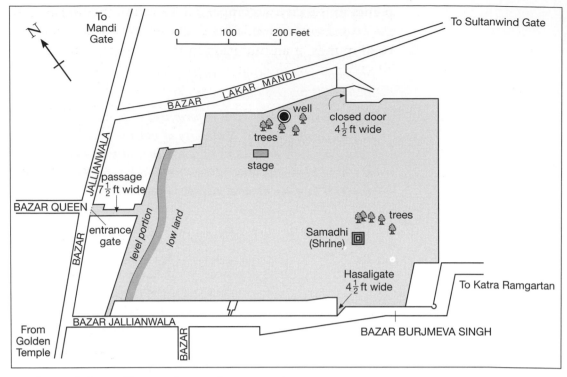

A plan of the Jallianwala Bagh in 1919

The Massacre

On the afternoon of 13 April, a meeting, started in the Jallianwala Bagh as planned. Estimates as to the number of people in the Bagh vary from 15,000 to 50,000, but there were certainly a lot and they were certainly unarmed. Some of them were playing cards, throwing dice, gossiping and generally relaxing in the warm sun; most, however, had come for the meeting. This began by passing two resolutions. One called for the repeal of the Rowlatt Acts; the other expressed sympathy with the dead and bereaved in the previous days' riots. Speeches were made and poems recited. Then the unimaginable happened.

The sound of heavy boots, marching at the double, was heard. Dyer, with Gurkha and Sikh infantrymen, appeared through the narrow passageway at one end of the Bagh. Without a word of warning, they knelt and, at a word of command from their British subaltern, fired and fired and fired again into the crowd. There was absolute chaos as thousands of people tried to escape and as they realised that they couldn't protect themselves and their families and friends. Altogether Dyer's men fired 1620 rounds of ammunition in ten to fifteen minutes, killing nearly 400 people and leaving a further 1500 wounded. Then, just as suddenly, Dyer and his men wheeled round and departed. They left the injured to fend for themselves or wait for help from family and friends brave enough to risk the curfew.

Sadar Partap Singh, who was not at the meeting but who knew his son was, rushed to the scene. This is how, later, he described what he saw:

I did not enter the Bagh from the side where the soldiers had come out because I was afraid, but went round and entered by jumping over a wall. A dying man asked for water. When I tried to take water from a pit, I saw many dead bodies floating in it. Some living men had also hidden themselves in the same pit. I went to find my son. There were 800 or 1000 wounded and dead lying near the walls and there were others who ran away wounded and died either in their own houses or in the surrounding lanes. I could not find my son. I heard wailing from those who had been shot and who were crying for water. Then I ran back home and heard my son was safe. I did not hear any proclamation forbidding people to attend public meetings.

Questions

3 How helpful is the plan of the Jallianwala Bagh in explaining why so many people were killed and injured there on 13 April 1919?

4 Would a historian consider Sadar Partap Singh's account to be reliable evidence about the aftermath of the Amritsar Massacre?

Martial law

Later that day, Dyer wrote an official report of what had happened and sent it to his superior officer, General William Beynon:

I entered the Jallianwala Bagh by a very narrow lane which necessitated leaving my armoured cars behind. On entering I saw a dense crowd, estimated at about 5000.

I realised that my force was small and to hesitate might induce attack. I immediately opened fire and dispersed the mob. I estimated that between 200 and 300 of the crowd were killed. My party fired 1620 rounds.

I returned to my headquarters about 18.00 hours. At 22.00 hours, accompanied by a force, I visited all my pickets and marched through the city in order to make sure that my order as to inhabitants not being out of their homes after 20.00 hours had been obeyed. The city was absolutely quiet and not a soul was to be seen. I returned to Headquarters at midnight. The inhabitants have asked permission to bury the dead in accordance with my orders. This I am allowing.

(Signed) R. E. H. Dyer, Brigadier-General.
Commanding 45th Brigade

Beynon's reply simply stated:

Your action correct and the Lieutenant-Governor [O'Dwyer] agrees.

Questions

5 In the context of Indian and British politics at the time, are you surprised by Dyer's report and the reply?

Secure in his superiors' approval, Dyer felt able to push forward with further harsh actions. Using threats of further violence, Dyer forced a stunned and grieving town to return to a semblance of normality. Shops and businesses opened and gradually people began to go about their daily affairs. Then Dyer declared martial law. But it was martial law that was aimed at humiliating the Indians who lived in Amritsar.

- Any Indian who passed Dyer or any other European had to **salaam**. If they did not, they were flogged, or arrested, or made to suffer indignities that were of immense significance to people locked into a system where caste, religion and social status were so important.

- In order to enable troops to move around the city, every means of transport was commandeered from the Indian population, including bicycles.
- All the Indian lawyers in Amritsar were forced to work as special constables and, in particular, witness floggings.
- All third-class railway tickets were withdrawn, making it virtually impossible for ordinary Indians to travel anywhere outside Amritsar.
- No more than two Indians were allowed to walk abreast on the pavements of Amritsar.
- The city's water and electricity supplies were cut off in the Indian quarters, causing great hardship to thousands of Indians.

Possibly the worse punishment of all, and which probably roused the Indians to even greater anger than the killings in the Jallianwala Bagh, was the 'Crawling Order'. Dyer decided that the Kucha Tawarian, the narrow lane where Marcia Sherwood was assaulted and left for dead, should become hallowed ground. He ordered that any Indians who wanted to pass along the narrow street had to crawl along it on all fours, in the muck and filth and general detritus that had collected there.

British soldiers enforcing the 'Crawling Order'

Dyer explained why he had invented this 'Crawling Order'

A helpless woman had been mercilessly beaten in a most cruel manner by a lot of cowards. She was beaten with sticks and shoes and knocked down six times. It seemed intolerable to me that some suitable punishment could not be meted out. Civil law is at an end and I searched my brain for some punishment to meet the case.

Dyer himself presided over a court in the Ram Bagh, where he meted out floggings and other forms of humiliating punishment to Indians found to be in breach of some element of martial law. He was not too particular whether the punishments went to the guilty or the innocent. What mattered was that the British Raj had to be seen to be in charge.

Details of what was happening in Amritsar began arriving in Britain. The Secretary of State for India, Edwin Montagu, was growing increasingly angry at the way in which martial law was being applied. The vast distance between London and Delhi, let alone Amritsar, meant that he never felt he had command of the whole picture. News could take weeks to reach him, and when it did, the situation on the ground had changed, rendering inappropriate any decision he was likely to make. Nevertheless, he was horrified when details of the 'Crawling Order' emerged. In the House of Commons he fumed:

> When you pass an order that all Indians must crawl past a particular place, when you pass an order to say that all Indians must salaam any officer of His Majesty the King, you are enforcing racial humiliation. When you take selected schoolboys from a school, guilty or innocent, and whip them publicly, when you whip people before they have been convicted, when you flog a wedding party, you are indulging in frightfulness. Are you going to keep your hold on India by terrorism, racial humiliation, and subordination, and frightfulness, or are you going to rest it upon the growing goodwill of the people of the Indian Empire?

Questions

6 What differences can be seen in the attitude of Dyer and Montagu to the 'Crawling Order'? What problems do they highlight for the effective governing of India?

The Hunter Committee

Pressed by the MPs in the House of Commons, and growing increasingly alarmed at the information filtering through from India, Edwin Montagu pushed ahead with his plans for an inquiry into the Amritsar Massacre. In a letter to the newly appointed Chairman of the Committee, Lord Hunter (former Solicitor-General for

Scotland) Montagu urged that the inquiry should be utterly fearless in its search for the truth.

On 11 November 1919 Hunter and his colleagues arrived in Lahore. Their job was to listen to evidence, ask questions and reach a conclusion about the events of 13 April. But nothing is that simple. As the witnesses arrived, they were alternately booed or cheered by the crowd; journalists, now that martial law, and with it censorship, had been lifted, had a field day. The trained lawyers on the committee tied many of the witnesses, including Dyer, in knots. Dyer admitted that he would have used the machine guns if he could have got the armoured cars into the Jallianwala Bagh; that he had not issued a warning to the crowd before opening fire; that he had continued firing until his ammunition was exhausted, regardless of the effect on the crowd; that he wanted to punish the Punjabis because they had been 'naughty boys'; that he had considered razing Amritsar to the ground. Dyer believed he had given his evidence truthfully. He had, and it was damning. In their report, the Hunter Committee roundly censured Dyer:

> *The action taken by General Dyer has been described by others as having saved the situation in the Punjab and having averted a rebellion on a scale similar to the Mutiny. It does not, however, appear to us possible to draw this conclusion, particularly in view of the fact that it is not proved that a conspiracy to overthrow the British power had been formed prior to the outbreak. General Dyer acted beyond the necessity of the case, beyond what any reasonable man would have thought to be necessary.*

The Committee's report also gently reprimanded O'Dwyer. Its three Indian members condemned them both.

The Indian View
The Punjab Sub-Committee of the Indian National Congress set up its own inquiry. It heard evidence in advance of the Hunter Committee and completed its report earlier. The Punjab Sub-Committee examined 1700 witnesses and published 650 verified statements. Their final report, including graphic photographs, amounted to a savage indictment of the way in which India was governed and was certain to arouse deep feelings of anger and

resentment among the Indian subjects of the British Raj. Their findings were unsurprising:

> The people of the Punjab were incensed against Sir Michael O'Dwyer's administration by reason of his studied contempt and distrust of the educated classes, and by reason of the cruel and compulsory methods adopted during the war, for obtaining recruits and monetary contributions and his suppression of public opinion by gagging the local press and shutting out nationalist newspapers from outside the Punjab ... The Rowlatt agitation disturbed the public mind and should be repealed ... the Jallianwala Bagh massacre was a calculated piece of inhumanity towards utterly innocent and unarmed men, including children, and unparalleled for its ferocity in the history of modern British administration.

Questions

7 What similarities and what differences are there between the reports of the Hunter Committee and those of the Punjab Committee? Does this make one of the reports more reliable than the other?

Discharge – but disgrace?

It was over. Dyer was summoned to Delhi and informed that the Hunter Committee had censured him, that the Viceroy's Council and the Commander-in-Chief agreed with them and that he had no choice but to resign. This he did.

As Dyer and his wife were supervising the crating up of their belongings for the long sea journey back to Britain, a deputation of European women presented him with an illuminated address 'on behalf of the ladies of the Punjab':

> We, the undersigned, desire to express our heartfelt gratitude for the firmness you displayed in the crisis which arose in this Province last April. We deplore the loss of life which occurred, but we believe it was your action which saved the Punjab and thereby preserved the honour and lives of hundreds of women and children. We trust, sir, that you will understand that we who would have suffered most had the outbreak spread, are not unmindful of what we owe to you.

WHAT DID CHURCHILL REALLY THINK?

Winston Churchill, the Secretary of State for War, supported Edwin Montagu in public. He did, in fact, believe that the Raj must rest on cooperation with its Indian subjects, and not on force, if it was to survive. In the case of Dyer and the Amritsar Massacre, Churchill privately thought that Dyer had been right to 'shoot hard' but could not accept Dyer's repeated assertions that he wished he had killed more Indians in the Jallianwala Bagh.

WHO CONTRIBUTED TO THE *MORNING POST'S* FUND?

All sorts of people contributed, from the very wealthy to those with modest means.

The Duke of Westminster contributed £100; Rudyard Kipling sent £10, William Gladstone, 10 guineas. A 'lady who was in Lahore' gave 10 shillings; Miss Lillie Faulkener sent a collection of antique coins. English-language newspapers in India sent cheques; two sisters sent four Queen Victoria Jubilee commemoration stamps and the £37 was collected at Alnwick livestock auction. Altogether £26,317 4s. 10d. was collected from the UK, India, the USA and Canada.

This view was supported by Miles Irving, a British official in the Punjab at the time of the massacre:

The whole rebellion collapsed. Not only the mob that was fired upon dispersed and all trouble ceased in the city of Amritsar, but also it was felt throughout the district. One of the reasons why there had been a danger was that the people not in the district thought for some reason or other that the Arm of Government was paralysed. The inaction of the police when the National Bank was burned lent some colour to that belief and there was an idea that the government could do nothing, and this came as disillusionment.

(Quoted in R. E. H. Dyer *Army Disturbances in the Punjab*)

Questions

8 Is it surprising that the views expressed here seem to be at odds with those of the Hunter Committee and Congress?

The entire garrison, officers and their wives, NCOs and sepoys, turned out to cheer Dyer and his wife and to sing 'For he's a jolly good fellow' as they boarded the train for Bombay. Large crowds, too, gathered on the quayside at Bombay to wish them well.

Controversy in the press

Dyer's ship berthed at Southampton on 3 May 1920. Immediately he was embroiled in controversy. Speaking to a *Daily Mail* reporter, Dyer insisted 'It was my duty – my horrible, dirty duty'. He reminded people that civil control of Amritsar had been handed over to him; no one in authority had condemned him for the massacre – on the contrary, he had been congratulated by his superiors. If he had done wrong, he insisted, as a soldier he should have been tried by a court martial, not asked to resign because a civilian committee censured him. The press and public opinion in both India and Britain took up entrenched positions. For some, Dyer was the man who had saved India. The *Morning Post* opened a fighting fund for Dyer and rapidly amassed £26,000 and presented him with a sword of honour and some much-needed cash. For others, he was the man who had brought disgrace to the Raj.

Arguments in Parliament

The controversy spilled over into Parliament, where a heated Commons debate on 8 July turned into more of a censure on Edwin Montagu, the Secretary of State for India. He argued that if Britain chose to rule India by the sword alone, it would be driven out by the united opinion of the civilised world. From the government benches, **Churchill** defended Montagu, stoutly denouncing the 'frightfulness' of the massacre, while the Ulsterman Sir Edward Carson argued that Dyer had stopped a revolution that was part of a global plot to overthrow the British Empire. Accusations and counter-accusations flew across the chamber, and in the end the government, with their motion to censure Dyer, held the day.

In the Lords, eleven days later, the debate went quite the other way. The motion 'That this House deplores the conduct of the case of General Dyer as unjust to that officer, and as establishing a precedent dangerous to the preservation of law and order in the face of rebellion' was carried by a majority of 43 votes. Of course the Lords' decision couldn't reverse that of the Commons, but many people saw it as a vindication of Dyer and his actions at Amritsar. Still others feared for its impact on Anglo-Indian relations.

An eminent Indian, Rabindranath Tagore, was in London at the time of the debates, and wrote home:

> *The result of the Dyer debates in both Houses of Parliament makes painfully evident the attitude of mind of the ruling classes of the country towards India. It shows that no outrage, however monstrous, committed against us by the agents of their government, can arouse feelings of indignation in the hearts of those from whom our governors are chosen. The unashamed condoning of brutality expressed in their speeches and echoed in their newspapers is ugly in its frightfulness. The late events have conclusively proved that our true salvation lies in our own hands.*

Tagore then returned the knighthood that had been conferred on him after he won the Nobel Prize for literature in 1913.

KEY PERSON

Motilal Nehru (1861–1931) Born in Delhi to a Kashmiri Brahmin family, Motilal Nehru was one of the first generation of young Indians to have a western-style college education in India. He became a barrister and settled in Allahabad, in the province of Uttar Pradesh.

Nehru's legal practice flourished and by 1910 he was leading a wealthy, westernised lifestyle and had emerged as one of the moderate leaders of Congress.

Gandhi and his philosophy had a tremendous impact on him, and Motilal Nehru became one of the first Congress members to abandon western dress and to try to limit his consumption of imported goods. Although initially close to Gandhi, and arrested several times for his participation in non-violent protests, he openly criticised Gandhi's suspension of the non-violent protests in 1922. He briefly joined the Swaraj Party, which aimed to put Indians in British-sponsored councils in order to wreck them, but this failed and he rejoined the Congress Party. Nehru chaired the Nehru Commission of 1928, which was intended to counter to the Simon Commission (see pages 94–98), and which proposed dominion status for India.

The entry of his glamorous son, Jawaharlal Nehru, into the Indian political scene marked the beginning of the Nehru political dynasty. The Nehrus became the most powerful political family in India, producing three prime ministers and were still controlling the Congress Party in the early years of the twenty-first century.

Questions

9 To what extent can the views expressed in Tagore's letter be supported by the evidence in this chapter?

EPILOGUE

Amritsar and its aftermath turned millions of loyal Indians against the Raj. They believed that Amritsar had revealed the true face of British rule and that any British reform that tended toward Indian independence was a sham. When **Motilal Nehru** presided over the Amritsar Congress in 1919, he warned delegates

> *If our lives and honour are to remain at the mercy of an irresponsible executive and military, if the ordinary rights of human beings are denied to us, then all talk of reform is a mockery.*

Ironically, a few days earlier, King George V had, by royal proclamation, enacted the Montagu–Chelmsford reforms. They would, he maintained, usher in a new era in Anglo-Indian relations.

CHAPTER 5

Gandhi, *swaraj* and the Congress Party

KEY TERM

Swaraj *Swaraj* means 'self-rule'.

In the years to 1914, Congress was a political party for the privileged few, supported by wealthy Indians. It most certainly did not have anything like a mass following throughout India. Congress debated issues, was consulted by various agencies of the Raj, and its members fell out amongst themselves. The most notable tensions were those between Gopale Krishna Gokhale, who believed Indians should respect the Raj and move slowly towards the distant goal of self-government, and Bal Gangadhar Tilak, who was prepared to use force to reach the same end (see pages 47–48) Yet by the early 1920s, Congress had become a political party with a mass appeal and a following of millions throughout India. It had sharpened its ideals and its demands and was tightly focused on independence. It was a force in the land and a force that the Raj could not afford to ignore. How had this happened? It had happened because of the hard work, vision and charisma of one man: Mohandas Karamchand Gandhi.

UNPROMISING BEGINNINGS

There was absolutely nothing in Gandhi's early years to make him stand out as a potential leader. Born in 1869 into a family who had for generations worked as minor administrators in the princely states, Gandhi as a young man was shy, awkward and had a poor command of English. Married as a teenager, Gandhi's family decided, in 1888, on the death of his father, to send the him to England to train as a lawyer. He returned to India as a qualified barrister, but failed to win cases as he was frequently too shy and embarrassed to speak out in defence of his clients. The offer of a year's contract with an Indian legal firm in South Africa must have come as a welcome relief.

HOW IMPORTANT WAS GANDHI'S SOUTH AFRICAN EXPERIENCE?

The time Gandhi spent in South Africa was of immense importance in both practical and philosophical ways.

Gandhi went to South Africa in 1893 and stayed until 1914. He worked there with the Indian community, gradually building up his skills and experience until he was their main spokesman in their struggles with the racial policies of the South African government.

Gandhi's work meant that he gradually built up experience and expertise through:

- working with a wide range of Indians from all castes, backgrounds and religions
- learning to cooperate and confront individuals in positions of authority in South Africa and in London
- learning about publicity by launching his first journal, *Indian Opinion*, in which he wrote about issues, rallied support and suggested coping strategies
- beginning to experiment with a variety of ways of protesting: marches, rallies, press campaigns
- experimenting with direct but non-violent opposition, such as burning registration documents.

It was this wide range of practical experiences that were to serve Gandhi, and the Congress Party, well on his return to India at the beginning of the First World War.

In philosophical terms, it was in South Africa that Gandhi began to develop his concept of *satyagraha* that permeated his philosophical and political writings, thoughts and actions from about 1907 until his death forty years later.

WHAT WAS GANDHI'S PHILOSOPHY?

Gandhi's philosophy was underpinned by his concept of *satyagraha*, a word he made up and which he used to describe non-violent resistance to injustice or evil.

It worked like this. Every single individual, Gandhi believed, was created to search for the truth. This truth permeated the universe and was present in the deepest part of everyone's being. In order to be fully human, each person had to reach that truth within themselves. Because every individual is at different points on their own personal journey to this truth, non-violence in relationships between individuals and groups of individuals is essential. This is because the weaker must not be forced to accept the views of the stronger against

KEY CONCEPT

Satyagraha This is a word made up by Gandhi and used to mean 'truth-force' or 'soul-force' and is applied to non-cooperation with the British authorities.

What is the difference between non-cooperation and passive resistance?
Gandhi hated the term 'passive resistance' and never wanted it applied to his methods. Passive resistance means just that – resisting authority by doing nothing. So sitting down in the street or tying yourself to railings would probably, depending on the context, be passive resistance. But removing your children from school and refusing to attend government parties would be an active way of resisting the Raj – by non-violent non-cooperation.

their own truth, no matter how weakly that truth is being held and sought. No one should be inhibited in his or her quest, and violence inhibits that search for inner meaning.

Were Gandhi's ideas in line with traditional Hindu philosophy?

It was the concept of *satyagraha* that set Gandhi's philosophy apart from traditional Hindu thought. Forms of self-suffering in order to change an opponent's mind were well known in Gujarat, just as passive resistance was well-known to Western thought. But for Gandhi and his followers, *satyagraha* was only for those strong enough in their commitment to truth to undergo suffering in its cause. It solved the eternal dilemma between means and ends, because *satyagraha* was both the means and the end. Those who carried it out became even stronger followers of truth; those against whom it operated were converted to a deeper vision of the truth. In all situations of conflict, Gandhi believed *satyagraha* could only generate truth and never falsehood.

HOW DID GANDHI BECOME LEADER OF CONGRESS?

Gandhi formed a strong friendship with Gokhale, who visited him in South Africa and who admired his work there. However, Gokhale was well aware just how out of touch Gandhi was with India and Indian affairs. He advised Gandhi to keep out of public life for at least a year while he found his feet and developed an understanding of the political dynamics in the country. Gandhi took this advice to heart when he arrived back in India in 1915.

Winning hearts and minds

He may have been out of touch with the complexity of current events in India, but this didn't stop Gandhi from having a very clear vision of the sort of society he wanted India to become, nor from creating a plan to achieve this.

Gandhi started from the premise that western technology had failed. It had not added to the sum total of human happiness and, indeed, had made man a slave to machines. In 1907 he wrote:

Formerly, people worked in the open air only as much as they liked. Now, thousands of workmen meet together and for the sake of their own maintenance, they work in factories or mines. Their condition is worse than that of beasts. They are obliged to work, at the risk of their lives, at most dangerous occupations, for the sake of millionaires.

Formerly, men were made slaves under physical compulsion. Now, they are enslaved by temptation of money and of the luxuries that money can buy. There are now diseases of which people never dreamt before, and an army of doctors is engaged in finding out their cures, and so hospitals have increased. This is a test of civilization. Formerly, special messengers were required and much expense was incurred in order to send letters; today, anyone can abuse his fellow by means of a letter for one penny.

Gandhi believed that people were much happier when they lived in small, self-sufficient communities. These communities would grow their own food, spin their own thread and weave their own cloth for their own garments. Freedom for India, he hoped, would be accompanied by the dismantling of the state and the return to small, simple communities of the past.

Of course, the idea was in many ways unrealistic. Bombay, Madras, Delhi and Calcutta were bustling

KEY THEME

The importance of spinning Gandhi believed that daily spinning would bring India's Indian leaders into closer contact with peasant life and enhance the dignity of labour in the minds of India's intellectuals who had never had to do physical work.

The spinning wheel – a *charka* – became the symbol of the Congress Party.

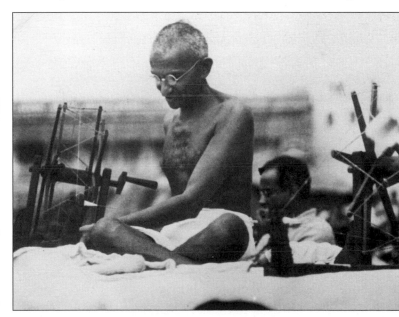

Gandhi spinning thread

modern cities, teeming with millions of people and couldn't possibly return to their rural origins.

BUT

- The idea of self-sufficient rural communities caught on and the Indian peasant masses began to take notice of Gandhi and to see in him someone with whose ideas they could identify.

Gandhi increasingly adopted a peasant lifestyle. He discarded the western clothes of an English educated lawyer and began wearing the Indian *dhoti*. This was a full-flowing cloth which men wore, covering the legs and which could be hitched up to look like a loin-cloth. Always a vegetarian, he began eating more and more frugally – again, as the Indian peasants did. And as the peasants did, he walked everywhere whenever he could.

No other Indian politician behaved like this.

- The Indian masses now began to identify, not only with Gandhi's ideas, but also with Gandhi himself. He looked and behaved like one of them.

There were those who realised how impractical Gandhi's ideas were. Arvind Nehru, a Cambridge-educated lawyer like Gandhi, became a judge under the Raj. He wrote in the 1920s:

> *Gandhi preaches that everyone must do without foreign goods and wear only the native-manufactured **khaddar**. So for interest's sake I sat down and worked this out the other night, only to discover that there would be something like three inches of kaddar per head of the population, and since even the loin cloth of my people requires more than this, lo, another distant Utopia!*

Gandhi rejected the lifestyle of Indians of his caste and profession, preferring instead to live in *ashrams*, austere communities of fellow believers and followers. This involved renouncing all sexual relationships as part of an individual's move towards purification.

- Gandhi had now identified himself with those traditional Indian beliefs that regarded the emission of semen as a loss of strength. Therefore not to indulge in the sexual act was a sign of power.

KEY TERMS

Khaddar This was cotton cloth produced in India.

Ashram A religious retreat or community built around a guru.

**Kasturba Gandhi
(1869–1944)** Kasturba was the daughter of a wealthy businessman, Gokuladas Makharji of Porbandar. She married Mohandas Gandhi in May 1882 when they were both thirteen years old. When Gandhi left to study law in England in 1888, she stayed behind in India with their newborn son, Harilal. They were to have three more sons: Manilal (1892), Ramdas (1897) and Devdas (1900).

In 1906, Gandhi decided to observe celibacy and he says Kasturda eagerly agreed to this. We do not know what she really thought. Nor do we know what she thought about the women followers who lived in *ashrams* with Gandhi and saw to his daily needs. We do know that, although she always stood by her husband, she found it difficult to accept all his ideas.

In 1897 Kasturba travelled to South Africa to be with her husband and from 1904–14 was active in the Phoenix Settlement near Durban. In 1913 she was arrested and spent three months in prison because of her protest against Indians' working conditions.

Kasturba travelled back to India with her husband. There her main role was to teach hygiene, discipline, reading and writing to women and children. She lived in *ashrams* with Gandhi. His autobiography records her refusal to join in all communal activities, like cleaning the lavatories, and there were also disagreements between them about what she saw as his neglect of their sons.

Kasturba died in 1944 from a severe heart attack following complications arising from *ashram* living, stress, pneumonia and bronchitis.

In these ways Gandhi associated himself with the mass of Indian people and acquired a vast following. His renunciation of contemporary values and society, and his search for the truth led to people calling him '**Mahatma**', which is usually translated as 'Great Soul'.

It was **Jawaharlal Nehru** (see also page 87), a member of Congress who worked with Gandhi from the earliest years, who explained what was happening:

> *He made rather astounding proposals asking, for instance, lawyers to give up their practice, and live simply and on next to nothing; everybody was to wear hand spun clothes made in the villages; and the whole atmosphere changed, and many of our older leaders were not quite clear what all this meant, because they'd been thinking differently. But he caught on so well with the Indian people, the masses, that older leaders were pulled then towards him. The fact that stood out about Gandhi was how he attracted people of different kinds and thereby he became a link between different groups from the poorest peasant, whom he always sought to represent, to princes and rich industrialists.*

Political manoeuvrings

Gandhi's outward humility convinced the leading Congress politicians that he was no threat to them. But Gandhi's moral values and vision for India's future meant that, in his view, he had to take part in the political process. He bided his time, and when he did move, did so cautiously.

- In 1917, he intervened in local situations, for example, where the peasant farmers of Champaran in north Bihar were forced by white planters to grow indigo on disadvantageous terms; and in Ahmedabad in Gujarat, where cotton mill-workers were earning a pittance. In Bihar, *satyagraha* took the form of his refusal to leave the district, and in Gujarat, he fasted until the situation was resolved. In both these cases, the positive outcome was probably due more to other political re-alignments than to Gandhi's *satyagraha*, but nevertheless his was an impressive performance.
- In the years 1917–18, Gandhi embarked on forging relationships with up-and-coming regional leaders,

such as the mayor of Ahmedabad, Vallabhbhai Patel; the Bihari lawyer, Rajendra Prasad and the young Jawaharlal Nehru. Gandhi was obviously developing an astute political awareness as to which people were likely to be of use to him in future struggles.

- He developed connections with two important communities that had largely been neglected by Congress politicians: Muslims and businessmen. This paid off hugely: the Muslims supported his takeover of Congress in 1920 and the business community pay-rolled his non-cooperation campaign. (See pages 85–89)

But not all the *satyagraha* campaigns went well. Horrified by the repressive nature of the Rowlatt Acts (see pages 63–4) which ordinary political protest and a unanimous vote in the Imperial Legislative Council had failed to stop, Gandhi called for a *satyagraha*. His idea was to hold a series of **hartals** throughout India, using this form of direct, non-violent action to break the impasse between politicians. It failed. *Hartals* were held, to a greater or lesser extent, in most of India's provinces. However, the degree to which they were observed varied from region to region, within and between provinces. More seriously, the stoppages erupted into violence in Gujarat and the Punjab. Gandhi immediately called a stop to the Rowlatt *satyagraha,* but even so that failed to stop the violence. It was a dreadful lesson. *Satyagraha* would only work if everyone involved understood its basic tenets and were not using it as a pretext to follow other agendas.

Viceroy Chelmsford wired to Secretary of State Montagu:

What a damned nuisance these saintly fanatics are! Incapable of hurting a fly, honest, but he enters lightheartedly on a course of action which is the negation of all government and may lead to much hardship to people who are ignorant and easily led astray.

What about the Raj?

When Gandhi left South Africa, he was not vehemently anti-Raj. Indeed, many of his speeches in the years 1915–18 were in support of British involvement in the First World War and of India's contribution to that

KEY TERMS

Hartal Stoppage of work consequent, usually, upon a workplace lock-out involvement. But three things led Gandhi to change his mind and to develop the idea of *swaraj*, or self-rule:

- the Rowlatt Acts, which aimed at continuing indefinitely the repressive wartime restrictions
- the Amritsar Massacre, and its tacit endorsement by large sections of the British community
- one of the outcomes of the **Paris Peace Conference**, whereby Turkey was to pay a huge indemnity and lose its colonial territories. This confirmed the worst fears of Indian Muslims – that white Europeans (and Americans) had little concern for Islamic nations.

By 1920, Gandhi had emerged as the leading politician in India.

- There was no other all-India political leader or group who could organise opposition to him. Gokhale died in 1915, Annie Besant was seen as a woman of little consequence and Tilak died in 1920.
- Members of Congress were so divided about which path was the best way forward that they couldn't unite to oppose Gandhi.
- Members of social and religious groups, who had previously exercised little influence at meetings of Congress, now appeared as delegates supporting Gandhi.
- There was wide geographical support for Gandhi because of the many local disputes with which he had been involved.

So it was that members of Congress had little alternative but to ally with Gandhi. They were prepared, provided they could influence its pattern and timing, to support Gandhi, *satyagraha* and *swaraj*.

HOW EFFECTIVE WAS GANDHI'S CIVIL DISOBEDIENCE CAMPAIGN OF 1920–22?

Congress's annual meeting, which in 1920 was held at Nagpur, was of immense significance. Gandhi dominated the proceedings and, by the force of his arguments, his ability to bind together Hindus and Muslims, and his sheer charisma, he persuaded the delegates to vote for his policy of non-cooperation with the British Raj. They did so by a majority of just over 2:1. Gandhi's aim was, quite

KEY EVENT

Paris Peace Conference
The First World War ended in November 1918 with victory for the Allies. A peace conference was held in Paris in 1919 to work out the terms of the peace treaties between the defeated Germany and the victorious powers.

simply, to make the Raj ungovernable. If this happened, Gandhi predicted that the Raj would wither and die within a year and *swaraj* would follow. It all seemed so simple.

What did non-cooperation entail?

Gandhi, and through him, Congress, urged all Indians to:

- boycott elections to the new legislative assemblies
- hand back all titles and decorations awarded by the Raj
- remove their children from government schools
- refuse invitations to social events put on by the Raj
- boycott the law courts
- withhold taxes
- refuse to buy imported goods
- leave all government posts.

Some of this was completely impractical. Most lawyers for example, were unlikely to want to abandon their lucrative practices and parents would not want to deny their children an education for an indefinite period of time. But many areas of non-cooperation were realistic and could quite easily cause the machinery of government to grind to a halt. Mass refusal to pay taxes, for example, would stop most government departments functioning.

From triumph to disaster

Gandhi, mindful of what happened to his earlier *satyagraha* campaign against the Rowlatt Acts, was terrified that the movement would again fall into the hands of the mob. Accordingly, he targeted those areas of government where Indian non-cooperation was unlikely to bring them into open conflict with the police. These, too, happened to be those areas, such as taxation and administration, that were vital to the functioning of the Raj. Here there were some initial successes. For example, students boycotted their examinations; taxes were not paid; a large number of qualified voters (up to 90 per cent in some areas) stayed away from the 1920 elections; around 200 lawyers stopped work; and during the visit of the Duke of Connaught to Calcutta in 1921, shops were closed throughout the city and very few Indians were present at official ceremonies of welcome.

KEY TERMS

Jihad A Muslim holy war

KEY PERSON

Jawaharlal Nehru (1889–1964) Jawaharlal was born and brought up in a wealthy Kashmiri household, the son of Motilal Nehru, who was a leading Indian barrister and leading Congress politician.

Jawaharlal had an English education: Harrow School and Cambridge University, where he read Law. He returned to India, where the Amritsar Massacre and the impact of Gandhi on Congress changed his life.

A popular orator, and deeply involved in the non-cooperation movement, he was in and out of prison in the 1920s and 1930s. He refused to compromise with the Muslim League and, through his negotiations with the British during the Second World War, was mainly responsible for the intransigence of Jinnah that led to Partition.

He became head of the interim government in 1946, and helped Louis Mountbatten negotiate the final stages of independence. He was India's first Prime Minister and remained so until his death in 1964.

Millions of Indians, however, were unable to understand the morality of *satyagraha*, and followed their own agendas, mostly paying off old scores and attempting to drive forward new initiatives. Violence broke out at different times and in different provinces. The Bombay *hartal*, for example, scheduled to coincide with the arrival of the Prince of Wales, turned into four days of looting and burning in which 53 demonstrators were killed and hundreds injured. In Rangpur, the mob attacked moneylenders. The muslim Moplah tribe of the state of Malabar declared a *jihad*, killing British people and wealthy Hindu and Muslim landlords and moneylenders, as well as forcing Hindu peasants and labourers to convert to Islam. In the Punjab and later in the Gangetic Plain, Deccan and other parts of India, Hindus forced Muslims to 'wash away their pollution' by total immersion in water tanks and rivers. Many drowned amid communal rioting and the always fragile Hindu–Muslim alliance was in serious jeopardy. *Satyagraha* was spiralling out of control and turning into Gandhi's worst nightmare.

Matters came to a head in February 1922, when Congress supporters in Chauri Chaura, a village in Gorakhpur, torched a police station and burned to death 22 Indian policemen who were inside. Gandhi immediately withdrew to his *ashram* to fast and meditate, emerging some days later to say

God has warned me that there is not as yet in India that non-violent and truthful atmosphere which alone can justify mass disobedience, which can be at all described as civil, which means gentle, truthful, humble, knowing, wilful yet loving, never criminal and hateful.

He immediately called an end to the *satyagraha*. His supporters were horrified. So much that was positive had been gained – why throw it all away because of a few outbreaks of violence?

As Gandhi explained to Jawaharlal Nehru:

I must tell you that this was the last straw. I was much disturbed by the Madras doings, but I drowned the warning voice. I received letters both from Hindus and Mohammedans from Calcutta, Allahabad and the Punjab, all these before the Gorakhpur incident, telling

Gandhi, swaraj and the Congress Party   87

me that the wrong was not all on the government side, that our people were becoming aggressive, defiant and threatening, that they were getting out-of-hand and were not non-violent in demeanour ... I assure you that if the thing had not been suspended we would have been leading not a non-violent struggle but essentially a violent struggle. It is undoubtedly true that non-violence is spreading like the scent of attar of roses throughout the length and breadth of this land, But the foetid smell of violence is still powerful and it would be unwise to ignore or underrate it. The cause will prosper by this retreat. The movement has drifted from the right path. We have come back to our moorings and we can again go straight ahead.

Gandhi was adamant. He turned away from political agitation and work on his 'constructive programme' which emphasised social welfare work in the villages along with, of course, hand spinning and weaving. This was back to basics indeed. Less than a month later, Gandhi was arrested by the British authorities and charged with *'promoting disaffection towards the government established by law'* to which he pleaded guilty and was sentenced to six years imprisonment. Was it all over?

Something lost and something gained?

Gandhi's idea that *satyagraha* could, of itself, bring about *swaraj* had been discredited, but Gandhi himself was clear that the concept wasn't wrong – what was wrong was that the Indian people were not yet ready for the sort of self-discipline that was necessary to make it effective.

One outstanding feature of Congress' commitment to *satyagraha* was the way in which members had involved themselves in peasant communities and had acquired a deeper understanding of peasants' needs. Peasants had hitherto been more or less ignored by members of Congress. For example, Jawaharlal Nehru was a member of Congress and became, like his father Motilal Nehru (see page 76), a barrister. He led a privileged life. In the summer of 1920 Jawaharlal made the decision to travel extensively in Awadh, in the heart of the province in which he had been born. This is part of his reaction to what he saw and heard there:

They were in miserable rags, men and women, but their faces were full of excitement ... Looking at them and their misery and overflowing gratitude, I was filled with shame, shame at my own easy-going and comfortable life and our own petty politics of the city which ignored this vast multitude of semi-naked sons and daughters of India. A new picture of India seemed to rise before me, naked, starving, crushed and utterly miserable. And their faith in us, casual visitors from the distant city, embarrassed me and filled me with a new responsibility that frightened me.

Allied to this was Congress' growing ability to understand and exploit local grievances and to link these, albeit not always successfully, with the broader campaign for *swaraj*.

What seems to have impressed Congress more than anything was the sense of excitement, of dynamism and the feeling that India was on the move – but to which destination?

CONCLUSION

By 1922 Gandhi was the undisputed leader of Congress. He had galvanised Congress members into setting the goal of *swaraj* and had given them *satyagraha* as the means whereby self-rule could be achieved. Yet Gandhi himself was something of an enigma. Obsessed with the totally impractical idea of an India composed of rural communities devoted to spinning and weaving their own cloth, he nevertheless inspired millions of Indians at all levels of sophistication to follow him and adopt his methods. The British Raj, which acknowledged it was dependent on the goodwill of the Indian people if it was to survive, would have to respond.

SUMMARY QUESTIONS

1 To what extent did Gandhi's experiences in South Africa equip him for the Indian political scene?

2 How far was *satyagraha* a sensible way of achieving *swaraj*?

3 Gandhi's vision of an Indian society consisting of self-sufficient rural communities was clearly unworkable in the twentieth-century world. Why, then, did so many Indian politicians support him?

4 'Gandhi's emergence as leader of Congress was carefully calculated.' How far does the evidence support this judgement?

5 How significant were the non-violent campaigns of 1920–22?

CHAPTER 6

Retrenchment in the 1920s

The 1920s, following the collapse of Gandhi's civil disobedience campaign on 1920–22, were largely a time of re-grouping and consolidation on the part of both the British Raj and Congress. This regrouping and consolidation, however, was for a purpose. The end of the 1920s saw lines of demarcation hardening, with a British government desperately striving to keep the Empire and the British Raj intact whilst at the same time conciliating Indian opinion. It also saw Gandhi attempting his most ambitious *satyagraha* yet and, alarmingly for the future, one from which the Muslims withdrew.

HOW DID CONGRESS CONSOLIDATE ITS POSITION IN THE 1920S?

Membership

During the period of non-cooperation, membership of Congress grew by leaps and bounds. From a base of 100,000 it rose to around 2 million by the end of 1921. True, some more conservative members left because they objected to seeing Congress turning from being a pressure group to one of open defiance to the British Raj; and a large number of Muslims left when non-cooperation collapsed because of what they regarded as Gandhi's failure to support them in their concerns over Turkey and the break-up of the Islamic Ottoman empire, but overwhelmingly the trend was upwards.

Congress had achieved this support by extending its appeal into geographical areas and wooing interest groups that had hitherto been neglected. Many of Congress's new supporters came from the richer peasantry and the commercial castes, but Congress was beginning to recruit support from railway workers, mill-hands and the poorer peasants, some of whom had organised themselves into peasant leagues.

Organisation

When Gandhi emerged as leader of Congress in 1920, the Party organisation consisted of three administrative levels: local branches, provincial committees and an All-India Congress Committee (the AICC). This structure was revitalised in 1920 because of Gandhi's perception that a new sense of direction and purpose was needed. Cooperation with the Raj was to end and was to be replaced by non-violent non-cooperation.

- Membership of the AICC was increased from 161 to 350, and seats were re-allocated on a regional population basis.
- Great emphasis was placed on recruiting from hitherto untapped groups such as trade unions and women.
- Around 100 additional provincial committees were set up and several hundred more local branches.

Gandhi set up a new unit within the AICC. This was the Congress Working Committee (CWC) and its job was to formulate policy. Gandhi used a clever analogy when he said 'The Working Committee is to the Congress what a Cabinet is to Parliament'. This was no idle comparison. Gandhi intended Congress to develop an alternative administrative structure that could take over when, as he hoped, the Raj withered away.

After non-cooperation

Non-cooperation collapsed in 1922 and, with Gandhi in prison, a seemingly leaderless Congress, with its strategy and tactics in tatters, might have been expected to fall apart. Far from it. Congress used the time as a breathing space within which to consolidate past successes and to expand into new areas.

While Gandhi was in jail, leadership of Congress passed to the moderates C. R. Das (a barrister in the Calcutta High Court) and Motilal Nehru. Both Das and Nehru favoured taking advantage of the Government of India Act of 1919 (see pages 60–61) and in 1923, members of Congress were allowed to stand for election to the councils set up by the Raj. In this way, it was argued, the Montagu–Chelmsford reforms could be effectively undermined. In fact, there was a totally different outcome. Many Congressmen were successful in local elections, and their presence on the local councils lent those bodies an air of respectability. It also lent an air of respectability to members of Congress and so increased the popularity of the Congress Party itself. Many middle-class Indians, alienated by Gandhi's campaigns, returned to the fold.

Gandhi, released from prison in 1924, went back to basics. He set up the All-India Spinners' Association, with the intention of spreading the word about hand-spinning and weaving, as well as promoting the more general cause of village self-sufficiency. He persuaded a willing Congress to embark on a programme of mass literacy and improvement of village sanitation. And Gandhi himself began to campaign vigorously on behalf of the 'Untouchables' to enable them to enter fully into Indian society.

Many millions of Indians must have breathed a collective sigh of relief. Gandhi appeared to have abandoned his confrontational programme of non-violence and Congress was emerging as a responsible political party, bent on improving the lot of the Indian people. How wrong they were!

Enter the 'young hooligans'

Many members of Congress would have been happy to let the process of constructive development continue almost indefinitely. But two events changed all this.

- Three energetic, charismatic young men, whom Gandhi was later to call 'young hooligans', burst upon the political scene.
- The British government set up the Simon Commission (see pages 94–97).

The two events were not unconnected.

Who were these 'young hooligans'? They were **Subhas Chandra Bose**, **Jayaprakash Narayan** and **Jawaharlal Nehru**. Together and separately they lobbied on the AICC and CWC relentlessly for renewed action – for another great push towards the goal of independence. Why did Gandhi label them hooligans? Because they were attracted to socialism, a doctrine they found fed

KEY PERSON

Jayaprakash Narayan (1902–1979) usually known as JP JP was born in Sitabdiara, a village in Uttar Pradesh. He completed his higher education in the USA, where he became a Marxist. After returning to India he joined the Congress Party and was arrested and jailed several times by the British for his participation in the independence movement.

After his release from jail in 1932, he helped form the Congress Socialist Party, a left-wing group within Congress.

Following independence and the death of Gandhi, JP led the CSP out of Congress and it became the opposition Socialist Party.

Originally a supporter of physical force to eject the British from India, JP was won over by the non-violence arguments of Gandhi and became a strong supporter of *satyagraha* as a tactic.

In 1920, JP married Prabhavati Devi, a freedom-fighter in her own right and close friend and disciple of Kasturba Gandhi.

their anti-Imperialist sentiments, and which Gandhi, deeply conservative at heart, regarded as dangerously radical.

Bose, Narayan and Nehru eschewed the idea of settling for dominion status, which had been floated immediately after the First World War and which had been discussed, on and off, by Congress ever since. This is part of an impassioned speech the young Nehru made to Congress in 1928:

> *I submit to you honestly that if I have energy to serve the country, that energy oozes out of me at the very thought of Dominion Status. I cannot go about spending my energy and strength for Dominion Status. I do submit to you that there are many like me in this country who feel like that. You will find in all India groups of organisations that are springing up full of energy and militant spirit and they promise to attain an early freedom for India. The question is, are you going to help the development of the militant spirit in the country? Are you going to help the development of this revolutionary spirit in the country or are you going to damp it and kill it in trying to bring about a compromise?*

THE SIMON COMMISSION AND ITS IMPACT

The Raj, too, drew breath after the collapse of the non-violent campaigns of 1920–22. British policy consisted of balancing the need to keep control at the centre while at the same time making concessions to Indian aspirations. The lines to be followed were those laid down by the Montagu–Chelmsford reforms (see pages 60–62). This meant that Britain retained responsibility for foreign policy and India's defence, and India's elected provincial and national assemblies took on responsibility for some financial and all social and welfare matters. A lot of good work was done by these assemblies, particularly in advancing cholera and smallpox inoculation programmes, despite Gandhi's opposition to them. Many Indians worked well with the Raj and had no problems in doing so, although a large section of Indian society regarded them as traitors.

GANDHI'S ATTITUDE TO VACCINATION

Gandhi regarded vaccination against smallpox as a manifestation of the evil that the British Raj had unleashed on India. Vaccination, he said, was a 'filthy process that is little short of eating beef'. He advised smallpox sufferers that they would be cured if they used enemas, made sure they ad plenty of fresh air, wrapped themselves in a wet sheet at night and changed their diet

What was the political situation in Westminster?

The British government had to be mindful, too, of the political situation in Westminster. The Government of India Act of 1919, which embodied the Montagu–Chelmsford reforms, was due for review in 1929. But 1929 was the year scheduled for a General Election. The Conservative government was worried that if the review was held after the General Election, and if the Labour party won the election, then policies on India would veer to the left. Labour Party politicians had strong links with Congress and Conservative party politicians were afraid that any review undertaken under a Labour government would give Congress more or less what they wanted. What was to be done? The Secretary of State for India, Lord Birkenhead, had the solution. He simply brought the review forward so that it happened before the General Election and under a Conservative government.

The Simon Commission

In 1927 the government sent a parliamentary delegation, headed by Sir John Simon, out to India to find out how

A demonstration against the presence of the Simon Commission

the Government of India Act of 1919 was working, and to make recommendations as to how, and indeed whether, it should be amended. The Labour MP Clement Attlee, who later led the Labour Party to victory in the 1945 British general election, was a member of the seven-man delegation. Significantly, there were no Indian members. The 'message' here was loud and clear. The future of India was to be decided by British politicians based in Westminster. Indians were to take no part in deciding their own future.

How was the Simon Commission received?

When the commission arrived in Bombay they were greeted by booing, jeering crowds carrying banners and waving black flags, shouting slogans like 'Simon, go home!' It was the same in Calcutta, Delhi, Lahore, Lucknow, Madras and Patna. Everywhere the Commission went they were met with mass demonstrations, which the police could barely control.

Indian opinion divided

A wide range of Indian political opinion was clearly opposed to the Simon Commission. Members of Congress, Hindu leaders, liberal thinkers and a large section of the Muslim League led by **Muhammed Ali Jinnah**, decided to boycott the Commission and refused to give evidence to its commissioners. On the other hand, Muslims from the provinces where they were in a majority decided to help the Commission's inquiries, as did a number of Anglo-Indians, Sikhs and 'Untouchables'. All of these minority groups hoped for a better future than that which they were anticipating under a Hindu-dominated Congress. However, the Simon Report, when it finally emerged in draft form, did little more than re-assert the status quo and was abandoned before publication. Events, as will be seen, had overtaken it.

The Nehru Report

The boycotters met in an All-Parties Conference, where a sub-committee produced a report, which was really the first draft of a written constitution for India. It was the work of two eminent lawyers: T. B. Sapru, a former law Member of the Government of India and, of course, Motilal Nehru.

KEY PERSON

Muhammad Ali Jinnah (1876–1948) Muhammad Ali Jinnah was born on 25 December 1876 into a family that was part of the prosperous business community of Karachi. Educated in Karachi, Jinnah went to England for further studies in 1892 and in 1896 was called to the English bar.

He started his political career by attending the National Congress in 1906. He was a member of the Imperial Legislative Council in 1909 until he resigned in protest ten years later. He joined the Muslim League in 1913 and the home Rule movement under Annie Besant in 1917.

Jinnah worked hard to create a situation in which Hindu and Muslim could together create a united, independent India. However, a widening gulf opened up between Jinnah and Gandhi on the subject of protecting the Muslim position and on Gandhi's civil disobedience programme. Resigning from Congress in 1920, Jinnah became the main spokesman for the Muslim cause within India.

When compromise failed, Jinnah pursued the separatist line on his return from England in 1935. In 1940 the Muslim League passed the Lahore Resolution, calling for a separate Muslim state somewhere in India. With Indian independence in 1947 came Partition.

Jinnah became the first Governor General of Pakistan in 1947, dying from cancer a year later.

The Report recommended **dominion status** for India on the same terms as those laid down for white self-governing countries within the British Empire and in which princely and British India were to be joined in a federation. There was to be no further devolution of power to the provinces. This meant, in effect, that Hindus would form a permanent majority within central government. Despite vague promises that religious freedoms would be safeguarded and new Muslim states would be formed, Muslims were deeply unhappy. Under the Nehru Report they would lose the protection of their separate electoral status perpetuated by the British as a result of the Lucknow Pact of 1916 (see page 58) The fragile Hindu–Muslim alliance, which C. R. Das, amongst others, had worked so hard to maintain, hung in the balance.

How did Congress react?

Congress, as has been seen, organised a boycott of everything to do with the Simon Commission as 'the only self-respecting course for India' and demanded immediate *swaraj*. Congress then took the initiative. At their annual conference, held in December 1928 under the presidency of Motilal Nehru, delegates backed two motions.

- They demanded instant dominion status (as recommended in the Nehru Report) even though one of the 'young hooligans', Jawaharlal Nehru, had grave doubts (see pages 93–94).
- Jawaharlal and Subhas Chandra Bose proposed a second, far more radical motion, which delegates also backed. This was that the British were to withdraw completely from India by 31 December 1929.

What if this didn't happen? Then a renewed campaign of total disruption would begin.

This was, of course, blackmail of the highest order and no one with any political sense would believe the British would comply. But it was also a clever political manoeuvre. The spotlight swung from the Simon Commission to Congress, and the British government would have to react.

The British response

In July 1929 a Labour government was elected in Britain, and their response was probably very different from that which would have been given by the Conservative government that sent the Simon Commission to India. The new Prime Minister, Ramsay MacDonald, was sympathetic to Congress' demands and so was the new Secretary of State for India, William Wedgwood. The 1920s had seen the ending of a long battle with Irish nationalists and the compromise of 1922; it had also seen the struggle for Egyptian independence end in an agreement that took account of Egyptian nationalist feeling. It had become clear that Ireland and Egypt could not be held by force and neither, then, could India. There was hope that some sort of similar settlement could be arrived at with India.

Lord Irwin, a Viceroy bent on conciliation, travelled back to England on his mid-term leave with two suggestions to put to the new Labour government: a conference to discuss future reforms and a declaration that the Raj's goal was dominion status for India. He met with a supportive response from both Ramsay MacDonald and William Wedgwood as well as, somewhat surprisingly, from Stanley Baldwin, the leader of the Conservative Party – a move that was to distance him from the right wing of his party, who were determined to keep India at whatever cost.

The Irwin Declaration, 31 October 1929

It was therefore with some degree of optimism that the Viceroy, Lord Irwin, issued what became known as the 'Irwin Declaration'. This reiterated the Montagu Declaration of 1917 (see page 60) and asserted that its 'natural issue' was to be 'the attainment of Dominion Status'. Thus, in so far as the British propaganda machine was concerned, there was absolute continuity in British policy towards India: dominion status was now officially the natural outcome of all that had gone before. Furthermore, Indian representatives were invited to London to a Round Table conference where details of a new Indian constitution would be hammered out.

The Working Committee of Congress officially welcomed the announcement, and called upon the British government to demonstrate its good faith by declaring an amnesty for all Indian political prisoners. This was a step too far for Irwin, who refused. Indian frustration at what they perceived as British stubbornness led to more terrorist attacks, including the bombing of the Viceroy's train and the destruction of the carriage next to the one in which he was travelling.

Gandhi's dilemma

Gandhi, like all the rest of the Congress leadership, knew that to attend the London Conference would be political suicide. Not only would they be on 'foreign' soil, but also they would be forced to follow the British agenda. What was worse, the British weren't just expecting representatives of Congress to attend the proposed conference. All representatives of Indian opinion were expected to be there: Sikhs and Untouchables, for example, as well as the princes, whom Gandhi regarded as nothing better than pawns of the British. The chances of Congress getting what they wanted would, Gandhi believed, be severely compromised. On the other hand, not to go to London would probably result in a settlement being made with which Congress – and Gandhi – could not possibly agree.

There was a second problem. Gandhi knew that despite the resolutions passed the previous year (see pages 96–7) Congress really was deeply divided in what to do about the Raj. Threats were one thing, action was another. Gandhi knew that to embark on another campaign of mass civil disobedience would alienate the moderates in Congress and could end up, as previous ones had done, in bloodshed and bitterness. On the other hand, the 'young hooligans' had considerable support in the districts, particularly among the young and the trades unionists, and were building up a steady following among younger Congressmen. Was Gandhi to back the young militants against the moderate conservatives and risk wave after wave of bloodshed, or was he to back the moderates, accept dominion status and risk dividing Congress for ever?

Congress decides

Added to Gandhi's problems in deciding the strategy and tactics that would get him what he wanted was the general problem of Congress' need to re-assert its authority. It was essential, given the proliferation of small groups that were finding a voice, for Congress to re-emphasise its claim to speak for all India. Not to do so would run the risk of allowing the British to settle with individual factions and in doing so, play them off against each other. Somehow, as many of the disaffected groups as possible had to be persuaded that to come under the umbrella of Congress was in their best interests. Somehow, a deeply divided Congress had to unite on the best way forward: cooperation with the Raj and Irwin's proposed Round Table conference, or non-violent confrontation.

Congress met in Lahore in December 1929. A policy decision could no longer be shelved. Gandhi had made up his mind: he would support the young militants. He steered his policy through the various Congress committees and a militant open session and ended up with a working committee of his own choice to direct Congress actions in the months ahead. Henceforward *purna swaraj* (complete independence) was to be India's new political demand. India stood poised for the next round of *satyagrahas*, due to begin on 26 January, which was designated Independence Day.

Risk-takers both?

Neither Gandhi nor Irwin was secure in the claims they made. Congress certainly did not represent the opinion of all India any more than Irwin had wide support for the strategy he planned.

THE SALT *SATYAGRAHA*

Congress had left it to their Working Committee to decide how and when the non-violent confrontation was to begin. They, in turn, decided that because Gandhi and his followers were committed to non-violence, they should decide.

Why did Gandhi choose to oppose the salt tax?

In many ways, deciding to oppose the government's tax on salt was the most sensible decision Gandhi could have made. Making salt was a government monopoly and the salt tax was a hangover from the days of the East India Company which brought in very little to the government – about 4 per cent of its total revenue. So the Raj was not likely to feel particularly challenged. The tax cost the average Indian 3 annas a year (about 1.5p) so there was no great issue there, either. But salt itself was an emotive issue: the one commodity everyone needed to make life itself sustainable, and the Raj controlled its production and exacted tax from its sale. What a symbol of power and oppression!

The march

Gandhi set out from his house in Ahmdebad on 12 March 1930, accompanied by a posse of reporters and camera newsreelmen. His intention was to walk the 240 miles (386 kiometres) to Dandi on the Gujarat coast. As he walked, thousands joined him, including, at his request, Untouchables, whose inclusion was supposed to demonstrate the universality of his mission. The march was a great publicity enterprise as the press dogged Gandhi's every footstep. Everywhere he stopped he preached the doctrine of non-violence and the world's press reported it faithfully.

On arriving at the coast in early April, Gandhi bathed and picked up a token piece of sea salt from the shore and India's female poet, Sarojini Naidu, shouted 'Hail, law breaker!' Gandhi issued a public statement confessing that he had broken the law and urged Indians everywhere to help themselves to the natural salt found in creeks and along the seashore. They did. Across India thousands of peasants followed Gandhi's advice and broke the law to collect the salt they needed in their daily life. It was a declaration of war against the tax and the government that collected it.

Across India hundreds of peasants were arrested and imprisoned. There were mass arrests, too, of national and local Congress leaders. Jawaharal Nehru was sentenced to six months' imprisonment on 14 April. In May, Gandhi

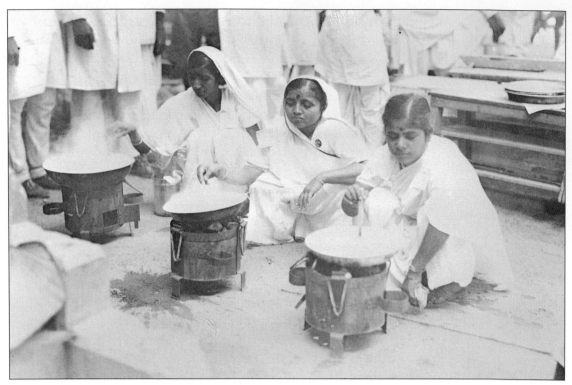

Some of Gandhi's followers boiling sea water to extract salt

himself was arrested and imprisoned. This sent shock waves throughout India, stimulating strikes and protests throughout the land. Particularly worrying for the government was the number of moderate men who seemed to be sympathising with Gandhi. In June, the entire Working Committee of Congress was arrested.

THE CIVIL DISOBEDIENCE CAMPAIGN

The campaign entered its second phase after Gandhi's arrest. Unlike the non-violent campaign of 1920–22, it was not masterminded and directed centrally. Provincial committees were authorised to organise their own *satyagrahas*. The nature and timing of the *satyagrahas* were to be determined by provincial imperatives, although Congress did recommend that the provincial committees should consider, in this order:

- salt
- a boycott of foreign cloth
- non-payment of taxes
- refusal to obey the authorities when they tried to prevent the *satyagrahas*.

In organising the civil disobedience campaign in this way, Congress cleverly papered over the cracks of potential divisions amongst its members as to just how disobedient civil disobedience should be. Furthermore, by allowing provincial committees such a large degree of autonomy, Congress hoped to demonstrate that it really was an umbrella organisation, sensitive to local needs. And, most important, the campaign was much more difficult for the Raj to stop because there was no central organisation to take out.

Was the campaign a success?

In 1930, the civil disobedience campaign became a formidable psychological weapon used against the Raj and, in places, an actual physical threat. By the middle of the year, all provinces in India had been affected, with Bombay and Gujarat being the most turbulent.

- In Bombay the Governor wrote of 'overt rebellion' and parts of the city became no-go areas for police.
- In the Bengal district of Midnapore, a salt *satyagraha* was followed by attacks on police and magistrates, intimidation of officials and a refusal to pay local taxes.
- In Bihar, an attack on the excise was catastrophic for government revenues.
- In the United Provinces, partly because of falling prices and oppressive landlords, a peasant campaign against land-tax was particularly successful.
- Local politicians in the Central Provinces decided to back opposition to forest laws, which forbade peasants to fell trees and graze their animals at will, ensuring that the wishes and needs of the local landowners were paramount in this respect.

In the majority of areas, civil disobedience was often used by people as a way of expressing local grievances, but these were expressed on the national stage and as such were impressive. Different groups were mobilised at different times and in different places. Civil disobedience became the vehicle whereby a whole range of people, from students to middle class businessmen, became politically aware and articulate. Women, in particular, became actively involved, often because their men-folk were imprisoned, but in their own right, too, and not as substitute males. By November 1930, nearly 360 women were in jail for their participation in different *satyagrahas*.

Order restored?

By early 1931, the Raj had, more or less, restored law and order. Official estimates say that around 60,000 people passed through India's jails in 1930. This had put an immense strain on the civil service, police and magistrates as well as causing intolerable overcrowding in the jails themselves. Indeed, by the end of 1930, there were still some 29,000 people in prison, most of them adult Hindu men, although around 2000 were youths under the age of seventeen.

There had been a point in mid-1930 when Viceroy Irwin had seriously considered imposing martial law on the most disaffected regions as the only way of keeping some kind of order. However, the memory of the disaster at Amritsar twelve years earlier, together with the belief that to bring in the army would be an admission of failure on his part, made Irwin keep his nerve. This paid off, because by the end of the year Congress was also feeling the strain. Local *satyagrahas*, whilst initially successful, could not always be sustained. Once local grievances had been expressed and settled, even if temporarily, life frequently returned to normal. Furthermore, there had been an economic slump early in 1930 and many had relished the opportunity to withhold taxes and the payment of bills. The economic upturn later in the year changed that, and the profit motive once again became paramount. People, too, simply ran out of energy and something like civil disobedience fatigue set in. By the end of 1930, the Raj and Congress were at stalemate.

The Gandhi–Irwin Pact

The only way out of the stalemate was some form of truce that would save the faces of Congress in general and Gandhi in particular, as well as of the Raj and enable them to move forward.

The end of 1930 saw Gandhi in prison developing his spiritual life, and Congress desperate to find some way of revitalising the civil disobedience campaign. Jawaharlal Nehru, released from prison in October, had the answer when he announced that the 'conquest of power' was about to begin. The authorities viewed this as a call to arms and open rebellion. He went straight back to jail.

Viceroy Irwin was afraid that Congress would find a way out of the stalemate by resorting to a campaign of violence. He wanted to create a situation in which Gandhi would be enabled to leave prison and participate in the London conference as the representative of Congress, yet Irwin couldn't be seen to negotiate openly with someone whom the authorities regarded as a terrorist. Furthermore, he had to be seen to support the ICS and those who had stood aside from confrontation. And, possibly the biggest hurdle of all, he had to persuade Gandhi that his presence at the Round Table conference was in Congress' best interest.

A meeting between Gandhi and Irwin was brokered by Indian businessmen, who were worried at the effect the civil disobedience campaigns were having on the Indian economy. They first approached Gandhi in July 1930, but it was only in February 1931 that Irwin and Gandhi met face to face. Irwin had done his homework and recognised in Gandhi both a spiritual being and a shrewd politician and was able to appeal to both sides of his nature. Indeed, Gandhi said of Irwin 'He desires peace because he has been touched by the struggle.' Discussions were frank and open, and helped by the fact that both men genuinely wanted to find a way out of the impasse. In the end, they were able to sign a pact.

- Congress's civil disobedience campaign was suspended.
- Gandhi agreed to attend a second London conference.
- 19,000 Congress supporters were released from jail.
- Confiscated property was returned to its owners.
- Some emergency restrictions were relaxed.

The Gandhi–Irwin Pact bought everyone a breathing space.

CONCLUSION

During the 1920s, Congress reviewed its position and was able to retrench and gather its strength to the extent that it was able to launch a nation-wide civil disobedience campaign at the end of the decade.

Significantly, very, very few Muslims took part in this campaign.

The Raj, despite making a serious mistake in the Simon Commission, was able to rethink its position, partly because of the election in Britain of a Labour government that was sympathetic to the cause of Indian nationalism. By 1931, the Raj and Congress had reached an agreement whereby Gandhi was enabled to travel to London to take part in the Round Table Conferences that were to determine India's future.

SUMMARY QUESTIONS

1   What were the main stages by which Congress became strong enough to mount a nationwide civil disobedience campaign in 1930?

2   Was the Simon Commission a big mistake? Explain your answer.

3   To what extent would you agree that Gandhi's decision to side with the 'young hooligans' in the meeting of Congress at Lahore in 1929 was a sensible one?

4   The Labour government of 1929 was sympathetic to the cause of Indian nationalism. Why, then, did 1930 see the beginning of a sustained all-India campaign of civil disobedience?

5   How successful were the civil disobedience campaigns of 1930–1?

CHAPTER 7

Jinnah, the Muslim League and the idea of separateness

Hindus and Muslims had coexisted in India for hundreds of years. There were always differences between the followers of each religion, but these worsened as the Indian people became more politicised at the end of the nineteenth and beginning of the twentieth centuries.

WHY DID HINDUS AND MUSLIMS CLASH?

The Hindu and Muslim communities in India were divided by their beliefs and practices that too frequently could find no areas of mutual toleration. The situation was exacerbated by the sheer size of the Hindu majority. Its size throughout India seemed to threaten the existence of the Muslim minority, which believed it had to fight, not only for its political voice to be heard, but also at some times and in some places for its very existence.

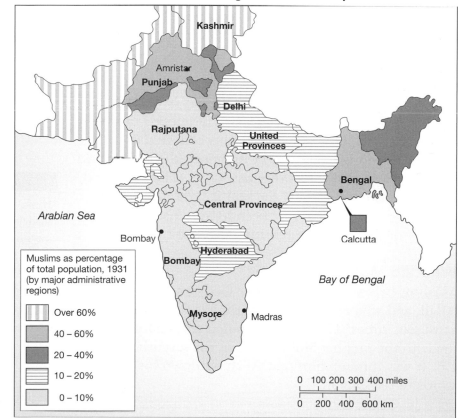

The distribution of Muslims in India in 1931

Muslims as percentage of total population, 1931 (by major administrative regions)

- Over 60%
- 40 – 60%
- 20 – 40%
- 10 – 20%
- 0 – 10%

0 100 200 300 400 miles

0   200 400 600 km

What do Hindus believe?

Hindus recognise one God, Brahman, who is the eternal origin and the cause and foundation of all existence. They worship him in a different way from the ways in which they worship other Hindu gods. This is because Hindus believe Brahman's work – that of creation – is done. The three principal gods Hindus worship all represent different aspects of him:

- Vishnu, the Preserver, who keeps the universe safe and his three important incarnations Rama, Krishna and Narasimha.
- Shakti, the Mother Goddess, who is also called Parvati, Mahalakshmi, Durga and Kali.
- Shiva, the Destroyer.

These divinities are frequently displayed in paintings and as statues.

Different Hindu communities had their own divinities whom they worshipped, but this was not in any way divisive. These were simply different ways of approaching the Ultimate. It therefore followed that Hindus did not have a problem with people worshipping other gods in other religions: they were all simply different routes to the same end. It also follows that Hindus do not have just one holy book, but several.

Hindu society was characterised by castes (see pages 15–16) which over the centuries had developed into a complex, hierarchical system. Hindus believe that everyone's soul is a tiny part of Brahman, the great world soul. The soul can be reborn many times. The body, and therefore caste, into which the soul is born depends on the kind of life that has just been lived. Existence is a cycle of birth, death and rebirth, governed by **karma**.

What do Muslims believe?

Muslims believe that there is one God, whom they call Allah, and who revealed their faith, **Islam**, to mankind at various times. The final and complete revelation was made to the prophet **Muhammad** in the seventh century CE. It was through him that Allah set down his holy words in the Qur'an.

HINDU HOLY BOOKS

Shrutis are the books of authority for Hindus. '*Shruti*' literally means 'that which is heard' because these scriptures were passed on by word of mouth.

The main set of texts is called the 'Vedas' and the parts of the Vedas that contain the philosophy of Hinduism are called the Upanishads.

The 'Bhagavad Gita' is a text that, although not part of the Vedas, is considered by most Hindus to be a text of authority.

'*Smritis*' are scriptures of lesser authority. They consist of historic stories such as 'Ramayana' and 'Mahabharata', mythological stories called 'Puranas' and law books like the 'Manusmriti'.

KEY TERM

Karma Karma is the sum total of a person's actions, especially their intended actions, that determine the state into which they will be reincarnated.

Islam The word Islam means 'submission to God'

Muhammad (570–632)

Born in Mecca, the son of a poor merchant, he was orphaned at the age of six and earned a living looking after sheep. Eventually becoming a merchant, he spent much of his time in solitary contemplation. When he was aged 40, the angel Gabriel appeared to him, urging him to teach the true religion.

The basis of Muhammad's teaching was the Qur'an which had been revealed to him by God. He attacked superstition, telling people to lead a pious, moral life and believe in an all-powerful, all-just and merciful God.

The Meccans rose up against him and in 622 Muhammad sought refuge in Medina, where he became the highest judge and ruler of the city. He then waged war against the enemies of Islam. In 630 he took Mecca and so was able to make Islam the religion of Arabia.

In 632 he made his final pilgrimage to Mecca and on Mt Arafat fixed the ceremonies of the pilgrimage (*hajj*) that all Muslims hope to make at least once in their lifetime.

The most important Muslim customs are the five obligations that that every Muslim must satisfy in order to live a good and responsible life:

- *shahadah*: sincerely reciting the Muslim profession of faith
- *salat*: performing ritual prayers in the proper way five times a day
- *zakat*: giving alms to the poor and needy
- *sawm*: fasting during the month of Ramadam
- *hajj*: making a pilgrimage to Mecca.

Carrying out these obligations provides the framework of a Muslim's life and demonstrates that they are putting their faith first and not trying to fit it around their secular lives. Different communities might insist on certain different practices, but at the heart lies the relationship between the individual and Allah.

Muslims do not believe in a caste system: there is no need for it because every individual has a direct relationship with Allah. Muslims do not, either, like to have or to see any visual representation of the Prophet Muhammad or of Allah. These are personal to them and too holy to be the subject of tawdry images.

The situation, of course, was not as simple as this. 'Hindus' and 'Muslims' were not two solid, monolithic one-dimensional communities. Within each community were significant differences and antagonisms between respective factions and schools of thought, for example between Shia and Sunni Muslims.

Could the two communities live together in the melting pot that was India? They had managed to do so more or less successfully for hundreds of years. Would pressure for Indian independence drive them apart or could some form of rapprochement be found?

What were common local points of friction?

It is clear that local communities were sharply divided by the very different belief systems held by Hindus and Muslims. These offered plenty of opportunities for irritation and petty disruption.

- Hindus liked to use gongs, bells and cymbals to create loud music when they were worshipping. Muslims preferred to pray in silence. Sometimes Hindus stopped playing music during the Muslim times of prayer and sometimes they did not. When they didn't, verbal abuse and violence resulted.
- Festivals were another source of friction. At the Muslim festival of Bakr'Id, cows were ritually slaughtered. But the cow was sacred to Hindus. On the other hand, the Hindu festival of Holi was particularly noisome and troubling to Muslims. It was a very jolly festival, lasting over two days. On the first day, bonfires were lit at night; on the second, people danced in the street, throwing coloured powder and water at each other and drinking a liquid laced with cannabis. There were plenty of opportunities here for irritation and mutual distrust to spill over into violence, and they frequently did.

At the beginning of the twentieth century an Englishman, Radclyffe Sidebottom, worked out of Calcutta as a river pilot on the Ganges. His greatest fear was that he would be accidentally caught up in Hindu–Muslim factional rioting:

The high-pitched screaming of the rioting crowd was something that you could never forget. You'd hear the screaming coming towards you. They would commit some horrible act and then patter away without a sound. But it wasn't so much the sounds, it was the smell of fear – and you'd get the smell of fear not necessarily from those who were being killed, but from the rioting mobs that were doing the killing. The moment the crowd decided that one of the opposite religion had been killed, then everybody in one form of dress would turn on the others and in a matter of forty-eight hours there were three hundred – four hundred – deaths. If you saw a man writhing in agony and you stopped you car and got out to help him – then you were finished.

Quoted in Charles Allen (ed.) *Plain Tales from the Raj*

The Hindu organisation Arya Samj was pro-active in the Muslim community in parts of northern India.

Members:

- openly criticised Islam and sought converts to Hinduism. Between 1907 and 1910 more than a thousand Muslims converted
- argued for the protection of cows, sacred to Hindus, and the established the Cow Protection Society. This brought them into open conflict with Muslim butchers and tradesmen;
- attempted to have Hindi replace Urdu as the language of administration. This frightened Urdu-speaking Muslims, who began to feel more and more threatened by the Hindu majority.

But it wasn't all one way. The Muslm *tabligh* and *tanzeem* (see page 112) movements were seen to be provocative by Hindus in the same way as the Arya Samaj was by Muslims

The situation was worsened when it became known that the major donors to the Arya Samj cause came from the Hindu merchant and moneylending class on whom lower-class Muslims depended for their economic security.

In 1915 a **Hindu Mahasabha**, was established that aimed to make the Hindu community powerful and independent. It was quite prepared to use force against people they thought were diluting the purity of the Hindu faith. It was a member of this group that was to murder Gandhi in 1948.

Was it the same throughout India?

From the late nineteenth century, the uneasy coexistence that had existed for hundreds of years seemed to be breaking down. This seems to have been partly due to the position of strict neutrality officially adopted by the Raj. This encouraged both Muslims and Hindus (and all other religions like Sikhism and Christianity) to believe that they had equal rights to carry out whatever religious practices were appropriate to their religion, no matter what offence they gave. Neither Muslim nor Hindu communities were prepared to consider compromise. More and more often, for example, Hindu processions were routed where they would cause most offence and disruption to Muslims going about their lawful business.

Some of the princely states experienced less Hindu–Muslim friction than those states that came directly under the Raj. This was probably because the governments of the princely states didn't feel it necessary to maintain a neutral position on matters of religion. They came down very firmly on one side or the other and everyone knew how much apparently extreme behaviour would be tolerated.

Did the Muslim community fight back?

Educated and upper-class Muslims responded by setting up organisations to counter Hindu dominance:

- In 1875 a Muslim leader, Sir Saiyyid Ahmed Khan set up Aligarh College where Muslims were educated and taught the English language so that they could better deal with the Raj and make their way professionally.
- In Lahore in 1885 an organisation was established to house and educate orphans so that they retained Islam and became good Muslims.
- A society was founded in Aligarh in 1894 for the preservation of Urdu.
- In 1906, Muslim leaders meeting in Dacca founded the All-India Muslim League (see page 53)
- In the early 1920s movements such as the *tanzim* and *tabligh* aimed to strengthen the Muslim community by weeding out all practices that encouraged greater understanding between Muslim and Hindu communities.

Less well-educated Muslims responded with violence, especially in areas where the Ayra Samj and the Cow Protection Society were active.

The deadly round of riot, violence, death, retribution and revenge was played out time and time again throughout India. It would take a massive amount of political and religious will to turn this around, and the will was not there in sufficient strength amongst enough people to make this happen.

HOW DID THE MUSLIM MINORITY IMPACT ON POLITICAL DECISION-MAKING?

The Muslims' main problem, politically, was that in every state they were in a minority. The map on page

107 shows this clearly. In the heady days of the Raj this had not been too much of a problem. As long as the governing élite ruled for the people, and political decisions were not made by the people, then numbers didn't matter too much. However, the situation changed radically once the Raj began tentatively to move towards a more democratic situation. Unless protected, the Hindu majority at every level could out vote the Muslim minority.

Education

There was a further dimension, unique to the Muslim community. Historically, Muslims had been slower than Hindus to take up the educational opportunities offered by the Raj. Consequently, by the beginning of the twentieth century, there was a considerable ill-educated and, indeed, un-educated Muslim underclass. The Muslim élite would never agree to this underclass having any sort of political control. As early as 1887 in a speech at Lucknow, Sir Saiyyid Ahmed Khan pointed out the problems:

> *Let us suppose that we have universal suffrage. And first suppose that all the Mahomedan electors vote for a Mahomedan member and all Hindu electors for a Hindu member. Now count how many votes the Mahomedan member has and how many the Hindu. It is certain the Hindu member will have four times as many because their population is four times as numerous. How can the Mahomedan guard his interests? It would be like a game of dice in which one man has four dice and the other only one.*

> *In the second place, suppose that the electorate be limited. Some method of qualification must be made; for example, that people with a certain income shall be electors. Now, I ask you, oh Mahomedans! Weep at your condition! Have you such wealth that you can compete with Hindus? Most certainly not. Suppose, for example, that an income of Rs. 5,000 a year be fixed on, how many Mahomedan electors will there be? Which party will have the larger number of votes?*

It seemed to be a no-win situation for India's Muslim population.

What sort of democracy?

Thus most Muslims, right from the start, strongly opposed any extension of democracy. In this they were tacitly supported by the more conservative members of the British administration. Congress, on the other hand, was increasingly pushing for the extension of the democratic principle of one man, one vote. How was this to be resolved?

Muslim leaders worked out a compromise position that was accepted by Lord Minto (see pages 47–52) when he promised that the Muslim 'rights and interests as a community' would be safeguarded. This compromise was enshrined, to the dismay of Hindus, in the Indian Councils Act of 1909 (see page 50) whereby the Muslims formed a separate electorate in order to protect their interests and for their voice to be heard.

How important was the formation of the Muslim League?

Initially formed in 1906 under the chairmanship of the Nawab of Dacca, the Muslim League was to be the voice of the Muslim community, an organisation complementary to Congress, which was dominated by Hindus. It is easy, with hindsight, to see a direct line from the formation of the Muslim League to the creation of the separate state of Pakistan. But in 1906 this was not a possibility considered by anyone in any position of power or influence.

Although conceived as an anti-Congress body, there were many instances where the League worked with members of Congress for the same outcome. In 1910, for example, the League, influenced by the Muslim 'Young Party' of Aligarh graduates and the vehemently anti-British seminary at Deoband in the United Provinces, moved to Lucknow and began discussing with Congress leaders the possibility of a joint nationalist programme. The outcome was the Lucknow Pact of 1916 (see pages 58–9) Significantly, the League's chief spokesman at the discussions leading to the Lucknow Pact was an active Muslim member of Congress, the Bombay-based barrister Muhammad Ali Jinnah. It is ironic that the creation of a separate Muslim electorate with reserved seats did not only allow Muslims a voice but also gave them an enhanced sense of Islamic identity that sat uneasily with the sincere secularism of men like Jinnah.

In December 1924, the League met separately from Congress for the first time since 1920, when Congress and League had joined together in protest against the Amritsar Massacre and the Rowlatt Acts. It planned a future for India that was based upon a loose federal structure, in which provinces would be largely autonomous and Muslims would continue to have separate electorates.

What was the importance of the Khilafat movement?

Events in the outside world impacted upon Muslims' perception of themselves as a political as well as a religious community. Muslims had long regarded the Sultan of Turkey as their Caliph, their most important spiritual leader. Turkey's decision to fight on the side of Germany, and therefore against Britain, during the First World War challenged Muslim loyalties to the extreme. The 1919 peace settlements did nothing to ease this tension as the Treaty of Sèvres greatly reduced the size of Turkey and removed the Sultan from power. The Khilafat Movement, set up to support the Caliph, spread rapidly throughout India. Using Islamic symbols to unite the diverse Muslim communities, it repudiated British rule in India and legitimised Muslim participation in the Indian nationalist movement.

Muslim leaders joined with Gandhi in mobilising the masses for the 1920 and 1921 civil disobedience and non-cooperation campaigns in response to the Amritsar massacre and the Rowlatt Acts (see page 65–77). At the same time, Gandhi endorsed the Khilafat Movement, thus bringing the weight of Hindu opinion behind what had originally been a solely Muslim movement.

Interestingly, Jinnah was opposed to Gandhi's support for the Khilafat Movement, believing that the Indian National Congress should not participate in religious matters.

Despite apparently impressive achievements, the Khilafat Movement collapsed.

- Turkey rejected the caliphate system of government, and became a secular state.

- The religious, mass-based aspects of the movement alienated western-orientated Indian politicians like Jinnah, who resigned from Congress.
- Many Muslims had become uncomfortable with Gandhi's leadership.

The precarious alliance of Muslim League, Khilafat committees and Congress collapsed once the non-violent campaigns ended. Congressmen began to regret the generous electoral arrangements agreed for Muslims under the Lucknow Pact and Muslims drifted away from Congress. By 1923 only 3.6 per cent of Congress delegates were Muslims; in 1921 the figure was 10.9 per cent.

THE PARTING OF THE WAYS?

Despite unpromising circumstances, Jinnah continued to work to try to bring Congress and League together to work out an agreed position for India's future.

Frank Mores, who knew Jinnah well, described him:

He was tall, thin and elegant, with a monocle on a grey silk cord and a stiff white collar which he wore in the hottest weather. Jinnah was one of the very few intellectually honest politicians I have known. Humility was not one of his strong points, but there was no humbug in his make-up. Like every decent-minded, thoughtful Indian he wanted his country to be politically free. The British completely misread the character and aims of this dedicated man. They had been accustomed to deal with a type of Muslim leader whose dislike for the Congress could be encouraged by official favours. But Jinnah had no purchase price.

This photograph of Muhammad Ali Jinnah was taken in 1947

At the 1927 meeting of the Muslim League, Jinnah persuaded members to make a bold offer to Congress in the hope of bringing Congress and the League back together again. Jinnah offered to end the League's support of separate electorates in exchange for a guaranteed third of the seats in the Central Legislative Assembly and the separation of Sindh from Bombay in order to create a Muslim-dominated province. The offer was rejected out of hand.

In 1929, Jinnah tried again. This time he offered a fourteen-point compromise plan. The main points were as follows:

- The future constitution should be federal, with the residuary powers vested in the provinces.
- In the central legislature, Muslim representation should be not less than one-third.
- Representation of minorities should be by separate electorates.
- Full religious liberty should be granted to all communities.
- The Constitution should embody adequate safeguards for the protection of Muslim culture.

This offer was, again, rejected. Jinnah despaired. Referring to the situation as the 'parting of the ways' he left for England and the English Bar.

In fact, the Muslim League and the Indian National Congress continued to negotiate right down to independence in 1947. But never would Congress receive a better offer for a peaceful settlement; never again would there be a Lucknow-style rapprochement.

CONCLUSION

The 1920s saw a hardening of the attitudes of the Muslim League and Congress. Despite apparent periods of rapprochement, both sides took up entrenched positions. Basically, Congress was unwilling to grant the Muslims concessions, such as separate electorates, that would guarantee their voice would be heard in whatever constitution emerged for an independent India. The Muslims would not accept a constitution that provided for anything less. By the end of the 1920s, Partition was beginning to become a real possibility.

SUMMARY QUESTIONS

1 To what extent did the fundamental religious differences between Muslims and Hindus mean that the two religions could not coexist in an independent India?

2 Why did the period of political rapprochement between Hindus and Muslims fail?

3 How far did the involvement of Muhammad Jinnah help or hinder the Muslim cause in India in the years to 1929?

4 By the end of the 1920s, had the establishment of a separate Muslim state in the Indian subcontinent become inevitable?

CHAPTER 8

Consultation and conflict in the 1930s

India did not gain its independence through one swift revolution, but rather through a process of evolution. The British government, the Raj, Congress and the Muslim League were the main players. Proposals were made, countered and adapted; sometimes they were adopted, sometimes they were thrown out and sometimes they were ignored. Individuals followed their own agendas; compromise did not always seem possible but sometimes broke a deadlock. And all this was being played out against a background of riot and repression, death and revolt in the Indian sub-continent. However, by the end of the 1930s, Indian independence was no longer a faraway dream: it was seen by both Indians and British as an achievable reality.

A QUESTION OF CONTROL.

India. "WHAT ABOUT CHANGING PLACES!"
John Bull. "WELL, YOU'RE WELCOME TO SEE WHAT YOU CAN DO AT THE WHEEL; BUT I THINK I'D BETTER SIT BESIDE YOU—WITHIN REACH OF THE BRAKE."

A cartoon, published in the magazine *Punch* in January 1931, sums up what most British people felt should be the relationship between Britain and India.

HOW SUCCESSFUL WERE THE ROUND TABLE CONFERENCES?

The **first Round Table Conference** (see page 98) was held in London in 1930. All shades of Indian political opinion were represented with the exception, of course, of Congress. Despite this, or perhaps because of it, considerable progress was made. It was decided that:

* India would be run as a type of dominion
* the dominion would take the form of a federation that would include the princely states as well as the eleven British provinces

- there would be Indian participation in all levels of government.

Between the first and second Round Table conferences, the British political situation changed. Lord Irwin, respected, conciliatory and liked, left India in April 1931 when his tour of duty came to an end. He was replaced by Lord Willingdon – a rigid Conservative who had earlier been Governor of Bombay and Madras.

Back in Britain, the first Labour government had been voted out and replaced by a Tory-dominated coalition cabinet facing a depression, unemployment and the collapse of the economy.

The second Round Table Conference, held in London in 1931, had a similar mix of delegates, but this time Gandhi was there, as the sole representative of Congress. In being present, Gandhi hoped to symbolise the unity of the Indian nationalist movement, insisting his attendance

The Round Table conference held at St James's Palace, London, in 1931

was 'with God as my Guide'. All it did symbolise was his arrogance in assuming he could alone represent such a vast and diverse organisation, and his lack of judgement in maintaining he could speak for India.

Frank Mores in *Witness to an Era* pointed out:

> *Gandhi made the fatal error of claiming to speak for the Muslims and depressed classes. The spokesmen of both communities repudiated him, and since the Muslims then numbered nearly thirty per cent of the population and the depressed classes about twenty per cent, it was difficult for him to sustain his claim that he represented 95 per cent of India.*

Indeed, Iqbal the Aga Khan (the spiritual leader of the Ismailis, a small Muslim sect) and Muhammad Jinnah attended the London Conference representing the Muslim League; Master Tara Singh the Sikhs, and Dr Ambedkar the Untouchables. All of them demanded separate electorates for their communities, and it was at this point that the London conference began to unravel. The well-known and well-rehearsed arguments began again, focusing on the desirability, or otherwise, of reserving seats for racial and religious minorities and how this would affect the resulting balance of power. Again, Hindus and Muslims could not agree and Congress had the additional worry of the position of the princes and the possibility of the emergence of an alliance between them and the Muslims that could outweigh any recommendations that might be made by Congress. Unsurprisingly, this second Round Table conference couldn't agree on a workable constitution.

The **third Round Table conference** was held in 1932. The British Labour Party did not send any representatives, and neither did India's Congress Party. Conference discussed the franchise, finance and the role of the princely states, but, again, could not reach any definite conclusions. It collapsed in 1933.

How did India react to the collapse of the Round Table conferences?

In India, the situation was deteriorating and Viceroy Willingdon decided to take a tough line. Lacking the temperament to engage in discussions with Gandhi, he followed the British government's instructions that he should conciliate only those elements of Indian opinion that were prepared to work with the current administration. As result of this the following steps were taken:

- On 4 January 1932, just one week after Gandhi returned to India, he was arrested and imprisoned.
- Congress was outlawed.
- All members of Congress's Working Committee and the Provincial Committees were rounded up and imprisoned.
- Youth organisations were banned.

Within four months over 80,000 Indians, mostly members of Congress, were in prison. Reaction on the part of the Indian population was swift but, in the absence of Congress leaders locally and nationally, and especially Gandhi, uneven and disorganised. Boycotts of British goods were common, and so was non-payment of taxes; youth organisations, although banned, became very popular; and terrorist activity increased, with more and more women becoming involved. Indeed, the United Provinces and the North-West Frontier Province became little more than armed camps and troops in Peshawar and Meerut were kept on armed alert. But by and large, the authorities kept control of the situation and the police never lost control of the streets or rural areas for very long.

Intervention from Westminster

In August 1932, Ramsay MacDonald, the British prime minister, announced his Communal Award, which was to be incorporated into any new Indian constitution. This designated Sikhs, Indian Christians, Anglo-Indians and Untouchables as separate classes, and entitled to separate electorates, as were the Muslims.

Gandhi was furious. He was not in favour of separate electorates anyway, but the inclusion of the Untouchables as a separate class was the final straw. The removal of the stigma of Untouchability had long been one of his missions and, in his mind, all Untouchables were Hindus. Thus, Gandhi reasoned, the British government was

KEY DEFINITION

Fast-unto-death. This was a common eastern way of registering a deep personal protest. An individual would refuse all food until they died. Sometimes a person would refuse water as well and this hastened death. However, most people adopting this dramatic form of protest would accept water because it made the process of dying take longer and so have more impact on their cause.

Other examples of hunger strikers are the suffragettes and the IRA internees.

Authorities hate this form of protest because they believe it creates martyrs. Usually at a loss as to what to do, they have swung from one extreme to the other, from force-feeding through to early release, and then to simply ignoring the situation and removing the individual to hospital at the point when the individual succumbs to organ failure. Their main object has always been to prevent an individual dying in prison.

further trying to weaken Congress by separating off the Untouchables as a group worthy of a separate electorate. He reacted in a dramatic fashion, launching a **fast-unto-death**. 'As a man of religion', he said, 'I have no other course left open'. Of course he had, but he chose in this way to persuade the government into withdrawing the Communal Award.

Neither Viceroy Willingdon nor Congress wanted Gandhi to die. Willingdon didn't want to make Gandhi a martyr and so, in his view, inflate the importance of his cause. He had plans in place to release Gandhi once he got to the point of no return so that at least he would not die in prison. Congress, of course, did not want to lose their iconic leader. In the event, Gandhi and Ambedkar, the Untouchables' leader, came to an agreement in Yeravda jail regarding the number of seats available to them on provincial councils (147 as opposed to the 71 allocated by the British government) and agreed that Untouchables would occupy 18 per cent of the Central Assembly seats as long as they ran for election by the general electorate. The British government accepted the Yeravda Pact; Gandhi ended his fast a week after it began, and the following week was celebrated as Untouchability Abolition Week. Although Hindu leaders declared that:

> *Henceforth, amongst Hindus, no one shall be regarded as an Untouchable by reason of his birth and will have the same right as other Hindus to use public wells, public schools, public roads and other public institutions.*

It took, however, another twenty years before Untouchability was abolished by law.

WHY WAS THE GOVERNMENT OF INDIA ACT PASSED IN 1935?

Back in the corridors of Whitehall, and faced with the apparent inability of the Indians to agree on their own constitution, British politicians set to and created one of their own. It wasn't that easy.

Opposition in Westminster

A determined group of Conservatives fought the Government of India Bill every inch of the way. They joined forces with ex-generals and former civil servants, some of whom had served in India, and together they formed the India Defence League. Rudyard Kipling (see page 25) was a vice-president and Winston Churchill its most vociferous supporter.

Churchill's views on India were formed when he had been stationed there as an army subaltern in 1897, and they hadn't changed since. He refused to accept that Indians were capable of running their own affairs:

> It is alarming and also nauseating to see Mr Gandhi, a seditious Middle Temple lawyer, now posing as a fakir of a type well-known in the East, striding half-naked up the steps of the Viceregal palace, while he is still organising and conducting a defiant campaign of civil disobedience, to parley on equal terms with the representative of the King-Emperor.

Media support for the India Defence League came from the *Daily Mail.* Its proprietor, **Lord Rothermere**, wrote a series of scurrilous articles under the general heading of 'If We Lose India'. These were laced with entirely erroneous 'facts' (Gandhi and Congress were 'a numerically insignificant group of 400,000 semi-educated babus who hanker after the spoils of minor office') and photographs of British troops quelling riots with lorries piled high with corpses. The message was clear: Indians were unfit to govern themselves and only the paternalistic British could effectively manage the subcontinent. If Britain were to leave India, carnage would follow. Furthermore, the *Daily Mail* warned, India was essential to the British economy and to lose India's trade at a time when every economy in the western world was struggling would be the height of folly. In fact, Churchill, taking up the tale of doom and gloom, was of the opinion that 'England, without her Empire in India, ceases to be a Great Power'.

Prime Minister Stanley Baldwin steered the bill through the Commons with quiet determination. He stuck to the position he had taken up when he supported the Irwin Declaration (see page 98) and never wavered from it. A pragmatic prime minister, he managed to convince the majority of his party that the British Empire was an

KEY PERSON

Harold Harmsworth, 1st Lord Rothermere (1868–1940) The younger brother of Alfred Harmsworth (who became 1st Baron Northcliffe), he became the business manager in the newspaper empire they founded.

A newspaper proprietor, he started by launching the *Daily Record* in Scotland, then bought out his brother's interest in the *Daily Mail* and finally the *Sunday Pictorial*. He controlled the Associated Newspapers group from Alfred's death in 1922 until 1932. He used this opportunity to write a series of articles supporting Hitler and Mussolini, defending the retention of the British Empire as a collection of dependent territories, and attacking Stanley Baldwin on the issue of Empire free trade.

organic organisation that had to change and develop, or die. In the Commons, the bill was attacked by Winston Churchill for giving away too much, and by Clement Attlee for not giving away enough. In the event, fewer than 50 MPs followed Churchill into the 'No' lobby and the bill became law in August 1935. The Secretary of State for India, Sir Samuel Hoare, acknowledging the furore created by the bill, countered by arguing 'No one in India has produced a workable alternative'.

WHAT WAS THE IMPACT ON INDIA OF THE GOVERNMENT OF INDIA ACT OF 1935?
The Government of India Act was the final British-written constitution to be imposed on India.

What did the Act say?
A Federation of India was proposed but never put into effect because the requisite number of states, mainly the princely bloc, would not join. Therefore only the clauses dealing with provincial governments were put into effect. The main features of these were:

- India was divided into eleven provinces, each of which had a legislative assembly and a provincial government. The provinces would control almost everything, except defence and foreign affairs.
- Each province would have a governor, who retained the power to act in an emergency.
- Dyarchy (see page 62) was abolished.
- separate electorates were to continue as before;
- Burma was separated from India and given its own government.
- Two new states of Sind and Orissa were created.
- The Viceroy would still be appointed by the British government and would be in control of defence and foreign affairs. He would have to follow the advice of an Executive Committee, which was made up mostly of Indians.

Why did both Congress and the Muslim League reject the Act?

Congress objected to the Act for several reasons.

- The Party wanted *swaraj* – full independence. Members were not interested in what they saw as a halfway house.
- Congress wanted a strong central government, which would inevitably be strongly Hindu, and not strong provincial governments, some of which the Muslims would probably be able to control.
- Congress also objected to the Act because it continued the practice of reserved seats for minority groups.

The Muslim League also objected to the Act.

- They believed it did not offer enough power to Muslims.
- Most provinces were controlled by Congress with no guarantee that the rights of Muslims would be protected.

The 1937 elections

Both Congress and the Muslim League were faced with an immediate dilemma: should they participate in the provincial elections, set for 1937? Not to participate would be consistent with their rejection of the Act, but the elections were going ahead anyway, and who knew what extremist group would achieve power? A total boycott would cut them off from government. Furthermore, to participate might give them the opportunity to work within the system to create change. Both Congress and League decided to take part.

How did Congress fare?

Congress virtually swept the board. The party gained overall control of the United and Central Provinces, Orissa, Bombay and Madras; and it became the largest single party in Assam and the North-West Frontier Province. Though fewer than half of the 1585 provincial legislative seats contested throughout India were open to the general electorate, Congress won them all, together with 59 more from the separate electorate contests, ending up with 716 legislative members. To all intents

The Lucknow Conference, 1936 This was the Conference at which Congress decided to participate in the elections. Jawaharlal Nehru explained their reasoning:

We go to the Legislatures not to cooperate with the apparatus of British imperialism, but to combat the Act and to seek to end it.

and purposes, Congress was a partner in government with the Raj.

How did the Muslim League fare?

In a word, badly. Jinnah only returned to India in 1935 from his self-imposed exile. He worked hard before the elections to build up a powerbase but in the limited time available to him, he wasn't even able to find enough candidates to contest all the reserved Muslim seats. An analysis of polling figures shows that Muslims gave little support to Congress candidates, even though they had to be Muslim to stand for the restricted seats. Indeed, the only overwhelmingly Muslim province that voted strongly for Congress was the North-West Frontier Province.

How did the Muslim League revitalise itself?

Jinnah realised that the Muslim League had two alternatives. It would have to attract mass support to enable it to win control in some provinces, especially the Punjab and Sind, where Muslims were in a majority, or it would have to enter into some kind of power-sharing agreement with Congress. Congress refused to contemplate this, and by doing so the Congress Party members played straight into the Muslim League's hands.

Many of the new Congress provincial council ministers, starved of power and recognition for so long, threw caution to the winds. They took advantage of their new offices and appointed relatives and caste brethren to jobs they had at their disposal. In some provinces, fiscal policies were drawn up to hurt Muslim landowners; in Bihar, cow-slaughter was banned; and Congress flags were hoisted on public buildings where there was a substantial Muslim minority. Now, as never before, many Muslims believed they needed the electoral safeguards that Jinnah and the League had long been demanding.

Jinnah rose to the occasion. He began a series of carefully orchestrated personal appearances, mass rallies and press interviews. The rallies and processions deliberately harked back to the glory days of the Mughal Empire with, amongst other memorials, a '**Tipu Sultan** Day'. But Jinnah and his spin doctors looked to the future too, as university students were deliberately targeted. Jinnah became the embodiment of Muslim identity, hopes and dreams. In spite of all the endeavours of Gandhi, Nehru and even Jinnah, Muslims could never be persuaded that the Hindu-dominated Congress party was their natural home. In the 1930s they turned to the Muslim League in their thousands. Jinnah (helped by Congress members) had at last given the Muslims a sense of identity and purpose.

There was one last-ditch stand to achieve Congress and League unity. Bose (see page 92) was elected Congress president in 1938. Jinnah met briefly with Gandhi, Nehru and Bose in that year, but talks broke down because of Jinnah's insistence that the Muslim League be recognised by Congress as the sole party of India's Muslims. Congress liked to think they were an inclusive party, capable of representing the entire nation. At the League session in Patna in December 1938, Jinnah reported that Congress had 'killed every hope of Hindu–Muslim settlement in the right royal fashion of Fascism'.

British officials watched with a kind of bemused bewilderment, mixed with satisfaction. Older men remained convinced that the British alone were best suited to running India. Younger men, like Maurice Zinkin of the ICS, believed that 'most accepted the inevitability of self-government at some time'.

Congress divided against itself

At the end of 1938, Congress itself was torn apart by in-fighting over its presidency. There was considerable pressure on Bose to quit: Gandhi didn't trust him and neither did the old guard. However, Jawaharlal Nehru refused to stand in his place and Bose himelf refused to step aside for the Gandhi faction's nominee, Pattabhi Sitaramayya. Bose knew he had the support of student, peasant and worker delegates and, in the first contested election ever for the presidency of Congress, won by 1580 votes to 1375. Twelve members of the Gandhi faction resigned immediately from the Working Committee in protest against the democratic election of their own president. Bose was left as president of a party

KEY PERSON

Fateh Ali Tipu (Tipu Sultan) (1750–99) The Muslim ruler and Sultan of Mysore, Tipu Sultan challenged British power by developing a new state and an army that could, and did initially, defeat the British.

Taught European military and administrative skills by French officers, he defeated the British at the Battle of Coleroon River (1782) and then negotiated with them to obtain recongnition as Sultan of Mysore. He turned Mysore into a strong and wealthy state by introducing new crops and industries (pineapples and silk, for example).

In 1789 Tipu attacked the adjacent British protectorate of Travancore. The resulting war ended humiliatingly for Tipu in 1791 when he lost half his lands to the British East India Company. He sought revenge by allying himself with the French, but even so the Mysore wars ended in defeat and his own death.

Tipu Sultan became a symbol of what Muslims, given the chance and the right conditions, could achieve.

that could not function because of a huge rift in its senior echelons. Gandhi ignored his pleas for help and Nehru's attempts at mediation failed. Finally, Bose was forced to resign and he was replaced by Rajendra Prasad, 'elected' by the Working Committee of which he was a member.

Bose and his brother Sarat Chandra walked away from Congress altogether. Back in their homeland of Bengal, they formed their Forward Bloc Party, dedicated to the revolutionary overthrow of the Raj.

Help needed
Throughout this period, between the passing of the Government of India Act in 1935 and its partial implementation in India up to 1939, the Raj experienced a brief period of popularity. More and more people, and in particular Congress chief ministers, looked to the administrative structures of the Raj for practical guidance and professional help on a daily basis. For Nehru, this was a source of deep depression; for all of the potential leaders, the realisation that freedom alone would not solve India's complex problems was sobering.

CONCLUSION
The 1930s did not see a dramatic change in the by now familiar pattern of proposal and counter-proposal, deadlock and riot. It saw little change in India's economic and social structure and little change in the daily life of India's teeming millions. But by 1939 a discernible shift had taken place. Indian independence no longer seemed to be an impossible dream but an achievable reality.

SUMMARY QUESTIONS
1 Who was to blame for the failure of the Round Table conferences?

2 How valid is the message of the *Punch* cartoon on page 119?

3 The Government of India Act (1935) generated considerable opposition in Britain and in India. How far was this opposition justified?

4 In December 1938, Jinnah claimed that Congress had killed every hope of a Hindu–Muslim settlement. To what extent was he correct?

5 Would you agree with the view that, by the beginning of 1939, the only obstacle to Indian independence was the Indians themselves?

CHAPTER 9

The impact of the Second World War.

The First World War (1914–18) had the effect of driving Hindus and Muslims together and so unifying India's nationalist movement. Events in the 1920s and 1930s, as you have seen, drove Congress and the Muslim League further and further apart, whilst at the same time making it more and more clear that India's independence from the Raj was achievable. The Second World War (1939–45) confirmed both of these developments: the ending of the Raj and the separation of Muslim and Hindu. It shattered all hopes of Congress and the Muslim League coexisting in an independent India.

HOW DID CONGRESS AND THE MUSLIM LEAGUE REACT TO THE OUTBREAK OF WAR IN 1939?

On 3 September 1939, Neville Chamberlain, the British Prime Minister, declared war on Nazi Germany. Lord Linlithgow, India's Viceroy, followed suit. On the same day, and acting (just) within his legal powers, he committed over 300 million Indians to war without consulting a single one of them. This, more than anything, demonstrated clearly that Britain still considered itself to be master in India. Had the previous 20 years been in vain?

What did Congress do?

The first reaction of Congress was one of shock and horror. What was the Government of India Act 1935 about if not some form of power sharing? How could the Raj behave as if India was still in the nineteenth century? This initial reaction was complicated by a feeling of deep sympathy with Britain in its struggle with European Fascism.

Gandhi urged the British government to negotiate with Hitler, using peaceful means, of course. Those members of Congress, like Nehru, who were at all familiar with events in Europe, knew just how futile this suggestion was. As hostilities commenced, Gandhi gave his wholehearted support to the British people:

> *We do not seek our independence out of Britain's ruin. That is not the way of non-violence.*

Nehru and other Indian socialists sympathised completely with the British approach to Fascism. They were not, however, prepared to commit themselves openly to support a government that had not consulted them prior to the declaration of war, nor – or so they said – were they prepared to fight unless they were granted immediate *swaraj*.

Congress' Working Committee passed a resolution:

> *A free democratic India will gladly associate herself with other free nations for mutual defence against aggression and for economic cooperation, but cooperation must be between equals and by mutual consent.*

In the early months of the Second World War, however, British politicians had other preoccupations, and demands for *purna swaraj* – complete independence – fell upon deaf ears. As a consequence, Congress' leaders ordered all Congress members to resign from provincial ministries throughout India. This was not necessarily the most sensible thing they could have done, since it removed hundreds of Indians from official positions where they had been in a position to mitigate the effects of war for their people and, to some extent, influence internal events in India. India's provinces reverted to a form of direct British government, something that they hadn't known since 1919.

What did the Muslim League do?

Jinnah could hardly believe his luck. Congress had, of its own volition, virtually retired from the political scene. The way lay open for the Muslim League to strengthen its position.

The last Congress provincial ministry abandoned its posts on 22 December 1939, as required to do by Congress leaders. Jinnah had earlier designated this day as Muslim

KEY CONCEPT

Pakistan The name Pakistan is an acronym of the names of the states that were to make up the new country: Punjab, Afghan Frontier, Kashmir, Sind and Baluchistan.

Put together, the whole word meant 'Land of the Pure'.

India's 'Day of Deliverance' and called on all Muslims to celebrate their release from Hindu bondage. This they did with gusto. Meanwhile, the League passed resolutions and offered prayers of thanks for 'deliverance from tyranny, oppression and injustice during the last two and a half years'.

There was no way back, now. The League worked with the Raj and the British government to support the war effort and to strengthen their own position within India.

The Lahore Declaration March 1940

Freed from the necessity of coping with Congress, Jinnah focused on the Muslim League and the challenging problems of formulating the League's constitutional goals – goals with which all Muslims could agree.

An estimated 100,000 Muslims gathered in Lahore in March 1940 and listened to Jinnah explain:

> *The problem in India is not of an intercommunal character but manifestly of an international one, and it must be treated as such. So long as this basic and fundamental truth is not realised, any constitution that may be built will result in disaster and will prove destructive and harmful not only to the Musalmans but to the British and Hindus also. If the British government is really in earnest, and sincere to secure peace and happiness for the people of the sub-continent, the only course open to us all is to allow the major nations separate homelands by dividing India into autonomous national states.*

Jinnah went further:

> *The Hindus and Muslims belong to two different religious philosophies, social customs and literature. They neither intermarry, nor dine together and indeed they belong to two different civilisations, which are based on conflicting ideas. To join together two such nations under a single state, one as a minority and one as a majority, must lead to growing discontent and the final destruction of such a state.*

The Lahore Declaration echoed the words of Jinnah, and was hammered out as a conference resolution on the night of 24 March 1940. It stated that:

No constitutional plan would be workable in this country, or acceptable to the Muslims unless it is designed on the following basic principles, viz., that geographically contiguous units are demarcated into regions which should be so constituted with such territorial readjustments as may be necessary that the areas in which Muslims are numerically in a majority, as in the north-western and eastern zones of India, should be grouped to constitute independent states in which the constituent units shall be autonomous and sovereign.

The League's Working Party was authorised to:

frame a scheme of constitution in accordance with these basic principles, providing for the assumption, finally, by the respective regions of all powers such as defence, external affairs, communications, customs and such other matters as may be necessary.

The word 'separate' had not yet been said, but the idea had been driven home relentlessly. The genie was out of the bottle. Jinnah could no longer see any possibility of a Hindu–Muslim rapprochement.

It is by no means certain that the Muslim League at this point envisaged that two separate states of East and West Pakistan would eventually emerge. However, the involvement of the eminent Bengali politician and strong proponent of a separate Pakistan, Fazul Huq, in the drafting of the Lahore Declaration makes it more than likely that this was a possibility in the minds of the drafters when they wrote of 'independent states in which the constituent units shall be autonomous and sovereign'.

The reaction of Congress

A battle of words between Jinnah and Gandhi ensued, with Gandhi maintaining that the Lahore Declaration was tantamount to the 'vivisection of India' and appealing over the head of Jinnah to the common sense of Muslims to draw back from the 'obvious suicide' that Partition would mean for India. Mini-*satyagraha* campaigns broke out and the perpetrators were jailed.

Nehru denounced the idea of Pakistan as a 'mad scheme' and toured India trying to strengthen the will of

Congress supporters. The young were already drilling and wearing pseudo-uniforms, ready for the supposed conflict with the Muslims. Nehru inspected one such body, carrying an imitation Field Marshal's baton, and was promptly thrown into jail for his trouble.

In reality, Congress was suffering from a self-inflicted wound: the withdrawal of Congressmen from positions of authority and influence in the provinces had completely weakened their hand politically.

THE THREATS TO INDIA

External threats

By the beginning of 1942, the Allies' position in all war zones was desperate. Hitler's armies controlled the Balkans and had invaded Russia; Rommel was within striking distance of the Suez Canal, and France had fallen to the Nazi onslaught as had most of Western Europe. In the Pacific theatre, Japan launched a lightening strike on the US naval base of Pearl Harbor in December 1941. The Japanese then swept through south-east Asia, and in a series of rapid strikes took Shanghai, Hong Kong, the Philippines, Malaya, Indochina and Thailand. On 15 February 1942, the 'unconquerable' island of **Singapore** fell. The whole of Asia now lay open to the Japanese. They pushed on into Burma, capturing Rangoon in March and Mandalay six weeks later. With Japan's declared aim of freeing Asians from European rule, Malays and Burmese welcomed the invading troops as liberators. The Japanese ships cruised at will around the Indian Ocean, once the unchallenged province of the British navy. Japanese forces were, quite literally, lapping at India's eastern boundaries.

Early in March, Viceroy Linlithgow confessed that he did not have sufficient armed forces in India to hold out against a Japanese landing on the Cuttack coast and could not prevent an advance into Orissa. All he could suggest, in response to a possible land invasion through Bengal, was a scorched-earth policy.

Bose: the enemy within?

In 1939 Subhas Chandra Bose (see page 92) left the Congress party and formed the Forward Bloc Party,

(see page 92)

KEY EVENT

The fall of Singapore 1942
Described as 'unconquerable', the island of Singapore, off the tip of the Malaysian peninsula, was taken by the Japanese on 15 February 1942. Part of the problem was that Singapore's huge defensive guns were all pointing out to sea and were useless against a Japanese invasion from the peninsula itself. Colonel Hunt surrendered his garrison of around 100,000 troops, who were taken prisoner by the Japanese. The Indian prisoners of war were later to form the backbone of Bose's Indian National Army.

Churchill described the fall of Singapore as 'the worst disaster and largest capitulation in British history'.

which was an organisation aimed at getting the British to quit India by any means. The organisation was banned by the Raj in 1941 and Bose fled to Afghanistan, finally ending up in Berlin. There his reception was lukewarm: **Hitler** feared that any collapse of the British Raj in India would lead to Russia moving in to the power vacuum created in the subcontinent, but Bose was encouraged to broadcast propaganda to India urging Indians to rise up against British tyranny. Finally, having no more use for him, the Nazis agreed that he could work with the Japanese on a possible land invasion into India. Bose was moved to Japan, where he formed the Indian National Army from Indian prisoners of war taken by the Japanese. Initially, Japan used the INA as a source of agents for behind-the-lines sabotage and spying in mainland India. Most of these agents were picked up by the Indian authorities, many became double agents and some simply took the train home.

KEY ATTITUDE

It seems that Adolf Hitler genuinely admired the Raj but was puzzled by the attempts made by the British to reach an accommodation with Indian nationalists. He once advised a startled Lord Irwin (then Foreign Secretary) that he should shoot Gandhi and as many Congressmen as necessary to 'make it clear you mean business'.

Wary of Indian nationalism, Hitler was afraid that the collapse of the Raj would leave a power vacuum into which either Russia or Japan could move. He held this view as late as 1942, when he refused to give even verbal support to Indian nationalism.

A cartoon, from an INA propaganda leaflet circulated in 1944, shows Churchill forcing a sepoy into battle, whilst behind him India rebels

Bose, however, still planned for a full-scale invasion of India. The Japanese, however, had more limited objectives, centred on a push against **Imphal**. In the spring of 1944, some 6000 soldiers of the Indian National Army went into action with Japanese troops. Of these 6000, some 600 deserted to the British, 400 were killed, 1500 died from dysentery and malaria and a further 1400 were invalided out of the war zone. The rest surrendered. It is believed that Bose, escaping in the last Japanese plane to leave Rangoon, died from burns shortly after the plane crashed.

Enter the Americans

The seaborne threat to India was only removed when the US navy defeated the Japanese at the Battle of the Coral Sea at the beginning of May 1942. The lesson was there for the world to see: a shift in power had happened. In future, India's seaborne security could only be guaranteed by the US, not the British, navy.

Early in 1941, before the USA entered the war, President Roosevelt and Prime Minister Churchill met on board the US cruiser *Augusta* in Newfoundland Bay and agreed the Atlantic Charter. This was basically an affirmation that all peoples should enjoy the right of self-determination when the war was over. Indian hopes were raised by what seemed like another commitment to their independence, only to be dashed when Churchill reassured the House of Commons that this did not, of course apply to 'India, Burma and other parts of the British Empire'.

When this was discussed in the Viceroy's Legislative Council, an Indian member, Jamuna Das Mehta, pointedly reminded the Viceroy that Indians were dying to bring freedom to others when that very same freedom was denied to them. Vinayak Savarkar, President of the All-India Hindu Mahasabha, appealed directly to Roosevelt, asking him to guarantee India's postwar freedom.

The US government, soon to become the senior partner in the war against Nazi Germany and the Axis powers, viewed the situation in India with some alarm. Roosevelt saw it as essential that India was swung fully behind the Allied war effort. True, thousands of Indian troops were fighting in the various theatres of war, but it was the situation within India that worried him. India simply could not fall to the Japanese, who had overrun the rest of south-east Asia. Furthermore, Roosevelt was very wary of committing American troops to fighting a war in Asia which could be seen as a last-ditch attempt to prop up the British Empire. Americans had not forgotten that they had formed part of the first British Empire, against which they had run a successful revolution in 1776.

Roosevelt began putting what pressure he could on the reluctant Churchill to agree to some form of self-government for India in order to unite the country. This was supported from within the British War Cabinet by Clement Attlee and Leo Amery, who were convinced that India's future safety depended on the creation of a popularly supported national government – not after the war, but immediately. This was not the same as self-government, but they were travelling in the same direction as Roosevelt. Churchill, cornered by colleagues on whom he depended, reluctantly gave in. He appointed the Lord Privy Seal, Sir Stafford Cripps, to lead a delegation to India.

WHY DID THE CRIPPS MISSION FAIL?

Sir Stafford Cripps and his delegation initially seemed to have many advantages. He was a Labour Party minister, a friend of Nehru and Gandhi, and personally sympathetic to Indian aspirations. Well-known and well-liked in Congress circles, he found much optimism on the Indian side when he arrived in New Delhi on 23 March 1942. Viceroy Linlithgow, however, was less than impressed, fearing that some sort of settlement would be imposed by the British government over his head.

But Cripps' mission was doomed. He came to offer a bargain.

- After the war, India would be offered full dominion status.
- The Indian people would elect an assembly which would frame a new constitution.
- If any province or princely state wanted to disassociate itself from the new India, it was free to go its own way.

And in return, because there are two parts to every bargain, all Indian parties were invited to join in an interim government of national unity under the Viceroy and his Council, which would operate until the end of the war.

Gandhi was furious. 'Why did you come, if this is all you have to offer?' he demanded of Cripps, 'I advise you to take the first plane home.' Congress rejected the first part of the bargain – they were not willing to accept a situation where states were allowed to opt out of a united India. They were, however, willing to join the proposed government provided it behaved like the Westminster one, with the Viceroy acting as prime minister and with the defence ministry under the control of an Indian. Churchill and Linlithgow were having none of it. The Raj had to remain in control while the war against Germany continued. Indian opinion was affronted, believing that this was yet another sign that Britain would cling on to India at all costs and would not accept Indians as equal partners. Jinnah, on the other hand, would have been ready to accept the Cripps' bargain, because of its implication that a separate Pakistan would not be a problem. However, he had to reject it too if the Muslim League was to remain part of the constitution-making process.

Cripps flew home on 11 April. Churchill had won a pyrrhic victory and Roosevelt had been wrong-footed. The Indians would not accept what had seemed to them to be a perfectly reasonable proposition.

WHAT WAS THE IMPACT OF GANDHI'S 'QUIT INDIA' CAMPAIGN?

In 1942, Gandhi launched his last great *satyagraha* campaign. On 3 May he declared:

> *I am convinced that the time has come for the British and the Indians to be reconciled to complete separation from each other. There is no common interest left to unite such distant and different nations.*

When asked by reporters to whom the British should relinquish their authority, he replied:

> *Leave India to God. If that is too much, then leave her to anarchy.*

Of the intervention of a deity we have no evidence; of a descent into anarchy, he was so very nearly correct.

What did Congress do?

Congress prevaricated. To commit to a *satyagraha* at such a critical time in Britain's struggle against Nazi Germany and the Axis powers seemed, on the one hand, like an act of great folly, even treachery. It would set Raj against Congress and make any reconciliation after the war (assuming an Allied victory, which in the dark days of 1942 seemed fairly unlikely) very difficult indeed. On the other hand, to remain quiescent now might give the upper hand to Jinnah, or to Bose. Congress had to make its position clear and had to rally its supporters to the cause of *swaraj*.

Finally, on 8 August 1942, Congress officially sanctioned Gandhi's *satyagraha*, his great 'Quit India' campaign. 'Quit India' was the shout that greeted every English man, woman and child as they went about their daily lives in India. 'Quit India' was shouted at the troops who were desperately trying to defend India's frontiers against the Japanese. Correctly guessing that the response of the Raj would be repression, Congress leaders, before they could be imprisoned and silenced, called on their supporters to make India ungovernable.

Congress versus Raj

Congress had spent three months arguing as to whether the Party should, or should not, support Gandhi's 'Quit India' *satyagraha* and the Raj had plenty of time to prepare contingency plans. On 9 August, the day after Congress officially sanctioned the campaign, Gandhi, Nehru and most of the Congress Party's leaders were arrested and interned. Within the next fortnight, thousands of local activists were rounded up and imprisoned. Offices were raided, files taken and funds frozen.

Gandhi, anticipating that this would happen, and realising that it would thus be impossible to organise the *satyagraha* from above, told his followers to 'Go out to die, not to live' urging every demonstrator to become their own leader. So began a horrific round of riots, killings, attacks on Europeans and damage to, and destruction of, government property. There were the usual targets: revenue offices and police stations but, alarmingly in time of war and with India daily expecting an invasion from the Japanese troops massing on its borders, stations and signal boxes were wrecked, railway tracks were torn up and telegraph and telephone lines pulled down. Over 1000 deaths and over 3000 serious injuries were directly attributed to the 'Quit India' campaign.

The Raj did not stand idly by.

- The threat to the transport of troops and war supplies was so great that on 14 August the RAF began flying sorties against the crowds threatening railway lines in the United Provinces and Bihar. They were ordered first to drop flares and, if that didn't disperse the crowds, machine-gun them. During one of the sorties, a plane crash-landed and two of its crew were murdered.
- 35,000 British troops were made available to support the police. Some were rushed between trouble spots; others guarded lines of communication, munitions stores and public buildings.

The authorities reckoned that they had about six weeks to get India under control before the monsoons stopped and a Japanese invasion could be expected from the east and a German one from the west and north-west.

Viceroy Linlithgow wrote to Prime Minister Churchill on 31 August:

> I am engaged here in meeting by far the most serious rebellion since that of 1857, the gravity and extent of which we have so far concealed from the world for reasons of military security. Mob violence remains rampant over large tracts of the countryside. I am by no means confident that we may not see in September a formidable effort to renew this widespread sabotage of our war effort.

Churchill, always an opponent of Congress, made his position clear to MPs in the House of Commons:

> We mean to hold our own. I have not become the King's first minister in order to preside over the liquidation of the British Empire.

Linlithgow may have been a little over-dramatic in comparing the situation to the Great Rebellion. In 1942, British Intelligence knew what was likely to happen and had forces waiting to be deployed. Raids on Congress branch offices yielded more information about the positioning of local disturbances. Undercover CID agents and informers had penetrated most of Congress' networks and as a result, Congress' room for manoeuvre was severely limited. In 1857 the Rebellion came as a terrible shock. The 'Quit India' campaign may have come as a shock, but the Raj was more than ready. Even so, there were brief losses of control everywhere.

- At Chinur, in Bengal, on 14 August, a crowd assembled to attack a police station, even though the ringleaders had been arrested a couple of days earlier. The local police inspector was murdered and two magistrats burned alive. Order was restored by 20 August by soldiers from the Green Howards. Afterwards, the soldiers were accused of murder and rape.

- At Sasaram, in Bihar, the railway line from Lucknow to Calcutta was attacked by a body of schoolchildren, university students and criminals. Local Hindu policemen refused to intervene because they were heavily outnumbered and order was only restored when a battalion of the Bedfordshire regiment arrived on the scene.

- At Ballia, in Uttar Pradesh, the outnumbered magistrate burned banknotes worth 400,000 rupees to stop them falling into the hands of the mob. Later, charred and burned notes were found to be in circulation.

- At Madhuban, in the United Provinces, local policemen had barricaded themselves inside their police station. Ranged against them were 4000 angry villagers armed with spears, saws, spades and two elephants. The stand-off lasted two hours and ended with the rebels running away. The defenders had fired 119 rounds and killed between 40 and 50 villagers. There were no police casualties.

By November 1942 the worst of the attacks were over. What, if anything, had been achieved?

BENGAL FAMINE 1943

The population of India grew by more than 50 million in the 1930s, with the rise greater in the north than in the south. The fertile lands of the Punjab could absorb the population increase, but Bengal, already densely populated, was struggling. The heavy demands of the army for foodstuffs during wartime, coupled with the restrictions on internal transport and the loss of imported rice from Burma, led to collapse. Grain merchants in Calcutta bought up all the rice they could from the peasants. This was rice that should have been kept in the villages for food and for seed for the next crop. The inevitable result was a terrible famine. At least 1 million people died from starvation, and some estimates put this figure as high as 3 million. Certainly, more Indians died in the famine, caused by the pressure of war and official incompetence, than were directly killed fighting in the war.

- Congress analysts showed that the 'Quit India' *satyagraha* had failed to paralyse the government, even in militant Hindu areas like Bihar. The reason they gave was that the military had remained loyal to the Raj. Even amongst Indian regiments, only 216 soldiers had gone absent without leave.
- The campaign had not attracted support throughout India in terms of geography, religion or caste.
- Non-cooperation had brought detention, despair and death.

HOW DID THE MUSLIM LEAGUE HANDLE THE WAR?

Back in 1940 Jinnah and the Muslim League had come out conclusively in favour of a separation of Hindu and Muslim after the war, expressed in the Lahore Declaration. Whether this was to be as a state within India, or as a separate country altogether remained, at that time, unclear. But the Muslim League's commitment to separateness had been openly stated, and the proposed Muslim state had been given a name: Pakistan.

Throughout the war years, Jinnah proved to be a much cleverer operator than either Gandhi or Nehru. He showed himself and the Muslim League to be prepared to co-operate with, and even support, the Raj, but without making any firm commitments. In doing so he pointed up the contrast between the League and Congress, providing the Raj with ample reasons to prefer to negotiate with the League.

The 'August Offer'

In May 1940, Linlithgow invited Jinnah to Simla, with the aim of discussing with him a whole range of issues relating to India and the war. Two months later, Jinnah submitted a list of tentative proposals to Linlithgow, which were welcomed. Linlithgow made the following proposals the basis of his 1940 'August Offer'.

- 'Representative' Indians would join his Executive Council.
- A War Advisory Council would be established which would include the princes and 'other interests in the national life of India as a whole'.

- An assurance would be given that the government would not adopt any new constitution without the prior approval of Muslim India.

The Viceroy accompanied this offer with a statement that seemed to place the Muslim League at the centre of any decision-making about the future of India:

It goes without saying that His Majesty's Government could not contemplate transfer of their present responsibilities for the peace and welfare of India to any system of government whose authority is directly denied by large and powerful elements in India's national life.

The message was clear. The wishes and needs of the Muslim community would have to be taken into account in any post-war settlement.

It was obvious that the vital role played by Muslims in the Indian army at home and abroad greatly strengthened Jinnah's hand, particularly when compared to what was perceived by the British government as being the obstructive attitude of Congress. The Secretary of State for India, L. S. Amery, complained to the House of Commons:

If only Congress could, in fact, speak for all main elements in India's national life then, however advanced their demands, our problem would have been in many respects far easier.

Here, indeed, was recognition of the fact that Congress did not speak for the whole of India, and an understanding that the millions of Muslims had to have their interests safeguarded.

The huge problem that remained for the British was not so much whether power should be transferred, but to whom?

CONCLUSION

The Second World War was in many ways a watershed. Before the war there was the possibility, however faint, that Hindus and Muslims could work out some sort of rapprochement. Afterwards, that possibility had gone.

During the war, Congress had shown that it still had control and influence over millions of Indians and that these Indians had irrefutably demonstrated that the Raj no longer had the consent of its Congress-supporting Indian subjects, and should go. The Muslim League had greatly strengthened its position, gaining tacit agreement from Britain that some sort of separateness for the Muslim community was possible, inevitable and even desirable.

The Raj, in turn, had demonstrated that it could hold India by force if necessary, and that it was more resilient than any had thought possible.

SUMMARY QUESTIONS

1 Why did Congress and the Muslim League react to the outbreak of war in Europe in 1939 in different ways?

2 To what extent was Gandhi's 'Quit India' campaign a mistake?

3 What was the significance of the Second World War in the fortunes of the Muslim League?

4 To what extent did the Second World War change the political situation in India?

CHAPTER 10

The Ending of the Raj

In June 1943 Field Marshal **Wavell** was appointed Viceroy, and remained in post until he was replaced by Mountbatten in 1947, whose charm offensive was supposed to smooth the way to a peaceful hand-over of power. It didn't work. The Raj's withdrawal from India after imposing partition resulted in terrifying rioting, mass destruction of property and the uncontrollable bloodletting and murder of thousands upon thousands of Hindus and Muslims.

WHY WAS THE BRITISH GOVERNMENT READY TO GRANT INDIAN INDEPENDENCE AFTER THE WAR ENDED IN 1945?

The ending of hostilities in 1945 saw Britain in an apparently contradictory situation. Outwardly, there was the image of a victorious nation. Unlike continental Europe, Britain had not been invaded; Britain was one of the 'Big Three' who had won the war and who would dominate peacetime reconstruction. Reality, however was somewhat different.

Changing economics

Britain was facing a desperate economic situation. Britain's industries, geared up to war-time production, had to wind down and change direction to meet the demands of peace-time. Furthermore, six years of war had drained Britain's financial reserves. Wartime debts had run at £70m per day towards the end and by 1945 the country owed £2,730m. On top of this, an enormous programme of reconstruction had to be undertaken, ranging from reforming the health and education services to rebuilding bombed and damaged ports, offices, factories and homes. Could maintaining an empire in India be afforded? Was maintaining an empire in India desirable?

There were many reasons why India was ceasing to be important to Britain, and many of the economic arguments for maintaining the Raj no longer held good.

KEY PERSON

Archibald Wavell (1883–1950) Wavell served in the Boer War and both World Wars as a soldier and administrator. After his 1941 counter-offensive in North Africa failed, he exchanged posts with Auchinleck to become Commander-in-Chief, India. Following the fall of Malaya and Burma to the Japanese, Wavell's main objective was to maintain India's boundaries to prevent a Japanese invasion from the east and an Axis one from the west. He succeeded.

It was made clear to him, on being made Viceroy of India in 1943, that his role was to hold the line: to keep India within the Empire and as a bulwark against the Japanese until the war ended and some kind of settlement could be reached with the Indians regarding their independence.

As Viceroy, he is best remembered for the measures he took to relieve the terrible famine in Bengal in 1943 and for the Simla conference of June 1945. Here he tried to bring about a rapprochement between Congress and the Muslim League, but failed. He hated the idea of partition, but came to regard it as inevitable.

Wavell worked hard to prepare the ground for independence and, ultimately, for partition. He was relieved of his post in March 1947 and replaced by Mountbatten, who oversaw the final months of the Raj and Indian independence.

- British investment in India had fallen during the 1930s and the shortfall had been made up by Indian capitalists.
- Indian imports from Britain had fallen dramatically. In the years 1928–9, Indians spent £83m on imported British goods. In the years 1935–6, this had fallen to £39m. High Indian import duties and cheap Japanese goods had squeezed out Lancashire cotton.
- In 1931 the Reserve Bank of India had been established. This meant that India could set the value of its own currency without reference to sterling.
- Indian troops had mobilised in the war against Japan, in North Africa and in Italy, and Britain had shouldered most of the costs. This meant that by 1945 the Indian government had built up a sterling balance in the Reserve Bank of India of £1300m because they had not had to meet the cost of their troops abroad.

Shifting loyalties

The old argument that Britain needed India as a bulwark of British power in Asia no longer carried much weight at a time when Indian politicians were protesting against the deployment of Indian forces in Indonesia and Indo-China. The politicians regarded it as unacceptable that 'their' forces were being used to, in their estimation, prop up decaying French and Dutch empires at a time when they were trying to free themselves from the grip of the Raj.

Two and a half million Indian men and women had joined the armed forces and by 1945 there were 15,740 Indian officers. But they were not all of them loyal to the Raj. Rather they were loyal to their concept of 'India' as their army commander-in-chief Auchinleck recognised:

> It is no use shutting one's eyes to the fact that any Indian soldier worth his salt is a Nationalist, though that does not make him anti-British.

The Indian Civil Service, too, had undergone a sea change. Originally the province of the British (see pages 35–7), by 1945 it was severely undermanned because of the need for able-bodied men to work in the armed forces and ancillary services. But even so, there were 429 British and 510 Indian ICS officers remaining in India.

So it would seem that, by 1945, neither India nor the British had much need for each other in an Imperial context. How, then, were they to extricate themselves from a situation in which they had once been mutually dependent?

POLITICAL MANOEUVERINGS

The ending of the Second World War and the prospects of elections in both Britain and India created a political situation that was temporarily unstable and one in which political manoeuvrings by the main players became evident as they prioritised their various agendas and prepared for the transfer of power from the Raj to India.

THE SIMLA CONFERENCE, 1945

In the spring of 1945, Viceroy Wavell travelled to London for a series of lengthy meetings with the British coalition government. The British Cabinet was ready, for two main reasons, to make a fresh attempt at an Indian settlement. Britain was millions of pounds in debt to India for goods and services borrowed to help win the war and this, combined with unrest in India, convinced Wavell and Secretary of State Amery that another attempt had to be made at a constitutional settlement. Wavell returned to Delhi with a new scheme, loosely modelled on that of Sir Stafford Cripps (see pages 132–133)

The major change Wavell was to propose concerned the composition of his Executive Council. This was to be chosen in a way that would give 'a balanced representation of the main communities including equal proportions of Muslims and caste Hindus'. Only the Viceroy and the Commander-in-Chief would remain British. From the outset, it seemed unlikely that Congress would be happy with this arrangement. Parity with Muslims would, in their view, inflate the importance of the Muslim constituency in India, and the phrase 'caste Hindu' implied that Untouchables were not Hindus.

Notwithstanding, a conference of Indian political leaders was held at Simla on 25 June 1945 to discuss the proposals. Congress leaders were released from prison so that they could attend, and in all some 21 Indian political leaders travelled to Simla, including Gandhi, Jinnah, Nehru – and Azad, the Muslim President of Congress, sneered at by Jinnah as a 'show case Muslim'. As could have been anticipated, Conference reached deadlock on the issue of how Muslim members of the newly reconstituted Executive Council were to be chosen. Jinnah insisted that they must all be nominated by the Muslim League; Congress could not accept such a restriction, maintaining that as Congress was an inclusive party, Muslims should be able to represent Congress as well as the Muslim League.

On 14 July, Wavell adjourned the Conference, without the deadlock between Congress and the Muslim League having been broken.

The British General Election
On 26 July 1945 the results of the British General Election were announced: the Labour Party had swept into power with a 12 per cent swing and 393 seats in the Commons as against the Conservative Party's 213. Nehru was jubilant at Labour's victory. He had always felt ideologically closer to Clement Attlee, the Labour party leader, than he had to the Conservatives. Just as there were new beginnings for Britain, there might, too, be radical changes for India.

The Labour–Congress Axis
Congress had, throughout the twentieth century, forged links with the Labour Party and with individual Labour MPs. It relied on the Labour Party to give voice to the opinions of Congress in the British press and the House of Commons, and it relied on personal friendships to enable this to happen.

Perhaps the most important friendship was that between Stafford Cripps and Jawaharlal Nehru. Both men were highly educated, highly intellectual and dedicated to radical reform of their respective countries. They gathered around themselves like-minded politicians who worked well together because of their shared ideals. One such man was Khrishna Menon, a London-based socialist who did much to create and maintain Labour–Congress links and who, at the same time, was a strong advocate of Nehru as India's future leader.

This rapport between Congress and Labour obviously made some things easier, but it created difficulties, too. The Muslim League had no such relationship with any British political party and within the ranks of their leadership there grew the strong suspicion that Labour was anti-Muslim. As events progressed, mutual suspicion took hold, and some Congress leaders became convinced that British administrators were leaking information to Jinnah.

Indian elections

The new British Cabinet's India Committee, dominated by Stafford Cripps, decided to recommend that elections should be held throughout India to allow people to choose their own representatives to a constituent assembly. This would give a clear indication of Indian opinion and pave the way for negotiations about a final political settlement.

The elections of 1945–6 gave Jinnah the mandate he had been looking for: the Muslim League won all 30 of the seats reserved in the Central Assembly for Muslims. Congress won 90 per cent of the general electorate seats. The fifteen remaining seats were divided among Sikhs, Europeans, and independents. This pattern was reproduced in the provinces. Congress retained control of Bombay, Madras, the North-West Frontier Province, Orissa and the United and Central Provinces. The League held Bengal and the Sind and, although it gained 79 out of the 175 seats in the Punjab, was kept out of power there by a combination of Sikhs, Hindus and the Muslim Unionist Alliance.

All this was carried out against a background of street violence, murder and mayhem. Indian National Army officers (see page 136) were being court martialled in Delhi's Red Fort; 7 million Indians were being demobbed from the armed services and were looking for work in industries that were laying off workers as they returned to peacetime production levels; drought threatened to produce famine in southern India and some sailors and their officers in the Indian Navy mutinied.

THE CABINET MISSION

It was into this maelstrom that Attlee sent his three-man Cabinet Mission to try to resolve India's constitutional problems.

What were the Cabinet Mission's proposals?

The 'three wise men', Lord Pethick-Lawrence (a peer with Liberal views), Stafford Cripps (now president of the Board of Trade) and A. V. Alexander (First Lord of the Admiralty and a Co-op sponsored MP) arrived in India on 24 March 1946. Attlee had insisted that the Mission did everything possible to maintain a united India – a united India that could play a key role in Britain's plans for security in Asia. This would seem to rule out a separate Pakistan, but did not preclude the existence, within Hindu-dominated India, of separate Muslim-dominated states.

The three men stayed in India for more than three months, determined to break the deadlock between Congress and the Muslim League. And they so nearly succeeded.

A second Simla Conference was held in early May, to which Congress and the League were each invited to send four representatives. The purpose of the Conference was to work through the Cabinet Mission's proposals. These, basically, provided for a three-tier federal structure within a united India. Partition was not acceptable.

The proposals were as follows:

- There would be an All-India Union, responsible for defence, foreign policy and internal communication, together with powers to raise finances to fund these three elements.
- The All-India Union would be governed by an executive and legislature.

- There would be three clusters of provincial governments:
  - (A) Congress' Hindu heartland of Madras, Bombay, Orissa and the United and Central Provinces
  - (B) Muslim and predominantly Muslim areas of Baluchistan, the North-West Frontier Province, Sind and Punjab
  - (C) Bengal and Assam, where the balance of religions was slightly in favour of the Muslims.
- Each provincial group would elect its own government to be responsible for the day-to-day running of provincial affairs.
- The All-India Union would comprise elected representatives from each provincial group.

This did seem to be the last and best hope of a peaceful transfer of power.

The Cabinet Mission concluded its proposals by stating:

We and our government and countrymen hoped that it would be possible for the Indian people themselves to agree upon the method of framing the new constitution under which they will live. Since this has not been possible, we have devised what we trust will enable you to attain your independence in the shortest time and with the least danger of internal disturbance and conflict.

The only alternative, they feared, would be 'A grave danger of violence, chaos and even civil war'.

Were the Cabinet mission's proposals acceptable?

Gandhi viewed the proposals with controlled optimism:

Whatever the wrong done to India by British rule, if the statement of the Mission is genuine, as I believe it is, it is a discharge of an obligation they have declared the British owe to India, namely, to get off India's back. It contains the seed to convert this land of sorrow into one without sorrow and suffering.

After a great deal of debate and prevarication, both the Muslim League and Congress accepted the Cabinet Mission's proposals. The League stated that they were acceptable because the basis of Pakistan was inherent in the Mission's proposals; Congress, convinced by its Muslim president, Azad, that the proposals were in Congress' best interests, voted to accept them and then promptly voted for Nehru as their president.

Stafford Cripps reported to the House of Commons that a breakthrough had been achieved. Cautiously optimistic, the Commons then turned to discuss a much more pressing issue: bread rationing in the UK.

Then Nehru scored an own goal. Or did he?

Snatching defeat from the jaws of victory

A few days after the Cabinet Mission's return to London, Jawaharlal Nehru held a press conference. Flushed with victory, and trying to woo the left wing of his party, he promised that once Congress controlled the All-India Union, it would act as it pleased. He predicted that the provincial groupings would fall apart because they were not liked by large numbers of Hindus and basically were only supported by the Muslim League. India would become, in effect, a Hindu Raj. The whole concept of Pakistan, Nehru insisted, would wither and die in the face of political reality. Alarmed, moderate Congress politicians tried desperately to limit the damage, but to no avail.

Jinnah was horrified. His worst nightmare was coming true. Nehru's comments were 'a complete repudiation of the basic form upon which the long-term scheme rests and all of its fundamentals'. Jinnah felt betrayed by Nehru and Congress – and betrayed by the Cabinet Mission, too, who had flown home, leaving him to deal with the collapse of what they had so carefully built up. Jinnah convened his council of the Muslim League in Bombay on 27 July 1946, and, denouncing the bad faith of both Congress and Raj, repudiated the agreement with the Cabinet Mission. Two days later, he called upon Muslim India to prepare for 'direct action'. 'Direct Action Day' was to be 16 August 1946.

WHAT WERE THE EFFECTS OF DIRECT ACTION?

It wasn't just Muslim India who were preparing for 'direct action', it was the Raj, too.

Commander-in-Chief Auchinleck, having made discreet enquiries among his Indian officers, found them to be loyal to their own concept of 'India' but privately warned Viceroy Wavell that he could not envisage Hindu firing at Hindu and Muslim shooting Muslim in any ensuing conflict.

Wavell had his provincial governors to worry about, too. Congress effectively controlled three-quarters of India. With the days of the Raj numbered, police loyalty would be swayed towards those who would inherit power and control. Wavell could not be sure he could contain the gathering storm.

16 August 1946

Never have we in the whole history of the League done anything except by constitutional methods and by constitutionalism. But now we bid goodbye to constitutional methods. We have exhausted all reason. There is no tribunal to which we can go. The only tribunal is the Muslim nation.

With these chilling words, Jinnah took India's Muslims into the horror and bloodletting of civil war.

In Calcutta, the police were ordered by the Muslim League to take a special holiday and the streets were given over to the mob. Within 72 hours, more than 5000 lay dead, at least 20,000 were seriously injured and 100,000 residents were homeless. Muslim and Hindu murdered each other in an orgy of killings and bloodletting, looting and arson that spread across India.

Wavell's appeals to Congress and the Muslim League to call a halt to the killings fell on deaf ears. Growing increasingly irritated by Gandhi, whom Wavell had come to regard as a malevolent manipulator, he was genuinely appalled when Gandhi remarked that if India wanted a bloodbath, she could have it. In similar tone, Jinnah had assured him that Pakistan was worth the sacrifice of 10 million Muslims.

Forming a government and losing a Viceroy

It was against this background of uncontrollable violence that Nehru was sworn in as prime minister of an interim government. Wavell finally managed to persuade a

Lord Louis Mountbatten of Burma (1900–79) A great-grandson of Queen Victoria and a close friend of the British royal family, Mountbatten was renowned for his charm, self-confidence, ambition and conceit.

Mountbatten had a spectacular career in the navy and in London society. In August 1943 he was made Supreme Allied Commander for south-east Asia and led the campaign to rid Burma and Malaya of the Japanese.

Known for his sympathies towards nationalist movements and for his slightly left-of-centre approach to politics, Mountbatten became Viceroy of India in 1947, charged with overseeing the transfer of power from the Raj to a responsible Indian government. The resultant Partition of the Indian subcontinent into India and Pakistan was accompanied by a horrendous bloodbath.

In 1949 Mountbatten resumed his naval career and was First Sea Lord at the Admiralty at the time of the Suez crisis (1956), over which he clashed dramatically with the Eden government. He was Chief of the Defence Staff from 1959 until his retirement in 1965.

In 1979 he was murdered by an IRA bomb.

The Commonwealth A loose federation of countries and states that once formed the British Empire. After the Second World War it became usual to refer to what had been the 'Empire' as the 'Commonwealth', the thinking being that in this way countries like Canada, which were largely self-governing, would have their status recognised and valued. To refer to them as 'colonies' was outdated and wrong, particularly when they had dominion status.

reluctant Jinnah to join the government. He did so only because he believed that the presence of five Muslim League members would be as good a means as any to pursue the goal of an independent Pakistan.

Wavell was worn out. He was having severe doubts about his ability to cope with the increasing strains that 1947 would bring as India moved closer to independence. It gradually became clear to Cripps and Attlee, partly because of Congress' wire-pulling behind the scenes and partly through their own dealings with Wavell, that a man with fresh ideas was needed to complete India's independence. Attlee wrote to Wavell on 31 January 1947, removing him from his post and offering him an earldom in recognition of his services to the Raj. Earlier, in the first week of January, **Admiral Viscount Louis Mountbatten of Burma**, had agreed to become India's last, and as it turned out, most controversial, Viceroy.

In the middle of February 1947, Attlee announced to the House of Commons that His Majesty's government had resolved to transfer power to 'responsible Indian hands' no later than 30 June 1948. By 'responsible hands', Attlee meant an Indian government that was capable of maintaining the peace. How was that to be managed?

The race was on.

WHY, AND WITH WHAT SUCCESS, WAS INDIA PARTITIONED IN 1947?

The brief given to Mountbatten by Attlee and the British government was clear. Partition was to be avoided; if Congress and the League couldn't agree terms by the given deadline, then Britain would devolve power to the existing central and provincial governments – and go.

Politicians, such as Ernest Bevin, the foreign secretary, together with the chiefs of staff, anticipated an attempt by Russia to expand into south-east Asia in the years after 1945 and viewed with foreboding the possibility of a prolonged armed conflict should this happen. In this event, Indian cooperation would be essential if Britain was to maintain effective contact, not only with the **Commonwealth** in the Pacific, but with the oilfields of the Middle East. This made the argument for a united

India even stronger: Auchinleck gloomily predicted that an independent Pakistan would need a British garrison to defend it against Russian encroachments through Afghanistan.

The 'charm offensive' begins

One of the reasons for sending Mountbatten to negotiate the final stages of India's independence was that he was totally different from any of the previous Viceroys. His flamboyance, left-wing tendencies and determination not only to be, but also to be seen as, a man of action brought a refreshing change to Indian politics and a hope that the Congress–League deadlock could be broken.

Mountbatten spent his first four weeks in India consulting with Indian ministers, politicians and his own staff. With some, his charm and flattery worked, as did his clear determination to cultivate the friendship of men with whom he had to bargain. Cordial relations were quickly achieved between the Mountbattens and Gandhi, Nehru and other Congress leaders.

By marked contrast, Mountbatten's first meeting with Jinnah was decidedly frosty. Jinnah was not in the least seduced by the charms of the Viceroy or Vicereine. Mountbatten was later to refer to him as an 'evil genius', a 'psychopathic case,' a 'lunatic' and, that old defamatory label, 'a bastard'. These epithets were duly relayed to Jinnah by staff who were trying to second-guess how events would turn out and where their loyalties should lie. This did nothing to improve Jinnah's view that Mountbatten had strong pro-Congress sympathies and this view was strengthened by the very clear and much-reported infatuation that **Lady Mountbatten** clearly held for the widower Nehru.

Lord Mountbatten was also the first viceroy to appoint a press attaché – the 1940s version of a spin doctor. The job of the man he appointed, Alan Campbell-Johnson, was to make sure the Raj ended in a blaze of favourable publicity.

Towards Partition

What Mountbatten heard during his four weeks of consultation made him believe that Partition was the

This carefully posed photograph of Gandhi with the Viceroy and Lady Mountbatten delighted Campbell-Johnson almost as much as it enraged Jinnah

only solution. This was most certainly not what Attlee wanted to hear. For the whole of its time in India, the Raj had tried to govern impartially between Muslim and Hindu and, indeed, one of its major successes had been that its rule was secular. To fall back, now, on a primitive division of a huge land-mass along religious lines was, so Attlee and his government believed, a seriously retrograde step.

So what had happened to make Mountbatten decide that Partition was the only answer? **Alan Campbell-Johnson** gave an explanation:

In his first talks with Lord Mountbatten, the Muslim League leader, Mr Jinnah, gave a frank warning that unless an acceptable political solution was reached very quickly, he could not guarantee to control the situation from his side. A similar warning was given by Congress leaders.

Unity had been Britain's greatest achievement in India, but by March 1947 the only alternatives were Pakistan or chaos. Lord Mountbatten discovered from personal discussions with the leaders of the Muslim League that they would insist on partition at all costs and fight a civil war rather than accept transfer of power to a Hindu majority union, while Congress showed themselves as champions of unity, but not at the price of coercion.

(From A. Campbell-Johnson, *Mission with Mountbatten*)

Death and destruction

Whilst Mountbatten was talking in Delhi, riots broke out in the Punjab. Although about 56 per cent of the Punjab's inhabitants were Muslim, it had been administered by a shaky alliance of Hindus, Sikhs and non-League Muslims under Khizr Hayat Khan. His resignation in March 1947, and the attempt by the League to form its own administration, led to militant Sikhs calling for direct action against the League – and the subsequent explosion of violence. Amritsar and Lahore were centres of carnage, while murder, arson and looting were common throughout the province. In the North-West Frontier Province, the League launched a civil disobedience campaign of its own against Congress.

What was Gandhi doing?

Gandhi was in despair. His dream of a single, united India in which all religions could coexist, seemed to be evaporating before his eyes. He fell back on his belief in the power of truth and love and began one of his long-distance walks. This time he walked through the Noakhali and Tiperah districts of East Bengal, trying though this 'act of love' to stop the mass killings that had left thousands dead. As always, he aimed to communicate directly with the illiterate masses, trying to explain what the politicians were doing. He then turned his attention to Bihar, where Hindus were killing Muslims on a large scale. As a practical gesture, it was a futile one. He had become an anachronistic figure and from this time on was sidelined in the search for an acceptable formula for independence.

Meanwhile, back in Delhi

Mountbatten and his staff were racing against the clock. Everyone involved, Indian and British, was exhausted, tense and sometimes bad-tempered. The momentum had to be maintained and the deadline had to be met. Ismay, Mountbatten's right-hand man, reported on 2 April that India was like a ship full of combustible material. The following months would show whether or not the ship would explode.

Plans for Partition

The plan for Partition, and the reallocation of power, was drawn up in April and May 1947.

Plan Balkan

The first draft, known as 'Plan Balkan', basically allowed the Indian states and provinces to decide their own future. This was a recipe for total anarchy, as past history had demonstrated, and as Nehru forcefully pointed out when the plan was unofficially and improperly revealed to him in a private meeting with Mountbatten. This was yet another example of Mountbatten's partiality – Jinnah had been given no such preview – but Nehru was essentially correct when he pointed out:

> *The inevitable consequence of the proposals would be to invite the Balkanisation of India; to provoke certain civil conflict and to add to violence and disorder; to cause a further breakdown of the central authority, which alone could prevent the growing chaos, and to demoralise the army, the police and the central services.*

Nehru went on to say that Congress would be sure to reject such a plan as it would both weaken India and also weaken the Congress Party itself. In the face of this, and mindful of Jinnah's constant and consistent refusal to accept any arrangement that would produce an impoverished Pakistan, Mountbatten and his advisers tore up 'Plan Balkan' and started again.

The final plan

In great speed and with no little embarrassment, Mountbatten and his staff cobbled together a new Partition plan. They were desperate to placate Congress and, at the same time, to get Jinnah 'on-side'. They were desperate, too, to get out of India before the subcontinent went down in flames. The remnants of the Raj were fast losing control of the domestic situation and Mountbatten was afraid the British would be swamped by events they could no longer control.

- Vast areas of north-west India were in a state of riot and rebellion.

- The 'steel frame' of the ICS, which had held India together in the heyday of the Raj, was now reduced to a mere skeleton of – mainly – Indians to whom their friends and relations looked for patronage.
- Attlee's declaration that the British would be out of India by July 1948 had led to bloody contests for supremacy in mixed Hindu–Muslim areas like the Punjab.
- The authorities' capacity for controlling the situation was severely compromised and collapsed altogether in Bihar.

Almost the only form of authority that could go any way towards holding the situation together was the army. And Partition would mean that the army would no longer be a national body, but Hindu would be split from Muslim, officers from men. When Viceroy Mountbatten, whom Auchinleck called 'Pretty Dickie', asked him how long it would take to split the army between Pakistan and India, Auchinleck replied two, possibly five, years. In the event, Auchinleck was given four weeks to complete the separation.

Jinnah, too, was in a hurry. His persistent cough and debilitating physical weakness had been diagnosed as symptoms of a terminal disease. If he wanted to see the birth of a separate Muslim state, events had to move fast.

On 18 May Mountbatten carried his plan for Partition, involving the complete separation of India and Pakistan, to London for government and then parliamentary approval. On 15 July, it was announced in the House of Commons that in precisely one month's time, two separate dominions of India and Pakistan would be created on the Indian subcontinent.

The Boundary Commission

The work of the Boundary Commission was to draw a boundary between India and Pakistan that would, as far as possible, accommodate Hindus and Muslims in separate states. The Commission comprised equal numbers of Hindu and Muslim judges (chosen by Congress and the League) and a chairman, Sir Cyril Radcliffe, who was a legal expert. His impartiality was guaranteed because he had no previous experience whatsoever of India; neither, his work being done, did he ever return. Using out-of-date maps, anecdotal stories of land ownership and dusty boundary charts, the Commission was given just five weeks to complete its work.

Rumours, leaks and pressure

With so much at stake, it was inevitable that some decisions were leaked to interested parties, who then applied what pressure they could to make the Boundary Commission change its collective mind. One of the worst offenders here was Mountbatten himself. A leak would reach Nehru, who applied pressure on Mountbatten who, in turn, attempted with some success to disrupt the Boundary Commission. This was certainly true in the case of Firozpur. The town controlled the only bridge over the River Sutlej as well as playing a strategic part in the irrigation system of the area. Radcliffe's first draft of the boundary in the area, flown to Lahore on 10 August, placed Firozpur firmly inside Pakistan, which resulted in intensive lobbying by Nehru and Congress to have the boundary moved. On the evening of 11 August, Radcliffe had dinner with Mountbatten and Ismay. The following day, Firozpur appeared on the Indian side of the boundary.

Mountbatten was certainly not acting in an even-handed way. This may have been due in part to his personal dislike of Jinnah and to the warm relationship Mountbatten and particularly his wife had with Nehru, but it was also due to the fact that Mountbatten simply didn't believe Pakistan would last. He likened it to a 'Nissen hut' that would soon collapse and be reabsorbed into India. It may have been this belief that led him to strengthen India at the expense of Pakistan.

What about the princes?

The princes had been unstinting in their support of the Raj during the Second World War. The Maharaja of Travancore had bought the Royal Indian navy an armed patrol boat; the Nawab of Bhopal bought fighter aircraft, as did the Nizam of Hyderabad, who bought a whole squadron of planes; and the Maharaja of Kashmir gave eighteen field ambulances. Altogether, the princes

MOUNTBATTEN'S ATTITUDE TO THE PRINCES

In private, Mountbatten was dismissive of the princes, calling them a 'bunch of nitwits'. He was bitterly critical of them for not accepting democracy and for not making an accommodation with Congress. In fact, most princes were, by 1945, making strenuous moves to turn themselves into constitutional monarchies.

invested in the war effort by buying 180m rupees-worth of war bonds. Of their subjects, 300,000 Indian volunteers had joined India's armed forces. Now, faced with the subcontinent being split between Muslim and Hindu, India and Pakistan, they felt ignored. Worse than ignored, they felt threatened by Congress, a party dedicated to removing their sovereign powers. As the Nawab of Bhopal remarked in 1946 'The British seem to have abdicated power and what is worse, have handed it over to the enemies of their friends'.

Later, he developed this theme in a letter to Mountbatten:

> *We wish to retain our relations with Great Britain, a monarchy, rather than to merge ourselves with an unfriendly political party which may tomorrow be ousted by Communist-dominated elements and which is almost certain to leave the British Commonwealth of Nations as soon as can be conveniently arranged. There is no guarantee of what the future Dominion of India will be. Are we to write out a blank cheque and leave it to the leaders of the Congress party to fill in the amount?*

Mountbatten took no notice of the Nawab of Bhopal and he took no notice of **Conrad Corfield**, the head of India's Political Department, either. He called a conference of Indian princes on 25 July at which he explained that when British paramountcy ended on 15 August, they should have acceded to either India or Pakistan, depending on which they were nearer to. By shamelessly exploiting his royal connections and playing on the princes' loyalty, fear and superstition, and by cajoling and flattering, browbeating and threatening, Mountbatten had them all signed up by the time of the transfer of power from the Raj to India and Pakistan. Many officials were outraged, believing the princes should have been given more time. An ICS officer in one of the states wrote of Mountbatten:

> *He applied the whole force of his immense prestige and his unique powers of persuasion to securing the assent of the rulers to new agreements that would permanently subordinate them to the successor governments of India and Pakistan. Except in the case of two or three States, the*

THE ACTIONS OF CONRAD CORFIELD

Conrad Corfield was the head of India's Political Department. He had little time for India's professional politicians and sympathised with the princes' desire to remain autonomous in their own lands and to keep meddling Congress politicians out.

Corfield got the new Secretary of State for India, Lord Listowel, to agree that neither India nor Pakistan would inherit the princely states when the Raj ended, but the princes would become, in effect, independent rulers. Having won this concession, Corfield authorised the burning of four tons of documents listing the princes' misdemeanours over the years. He wanted to prevent the papers from falling into the hands of Congress, the members of which, he suspected, would use them for political blackmail.

Nehru was furious when he heard of what Corfield had done. If carried through, it would mean the disintegration of India and a complete reverse for Congress, who intended quietly to take over the princely states. Mountbatten, who deeply resented being outwitted by an official, called Corfield a 'son-of-a-bitch' and had no problems in giving in to Nehru's demands that Corfield should be dismissed as 'an enemy of India'.

pressure that he exercised proved effective. The Princes of India signed their own death warrants and their States disappeared from the face of the map. Once allies of the Crown, they are now pensioners of a Republic.

In Dhrangadhara, the Maharaja remembered what happened when he explained the changes to the people in his state:

There was a stunned silence when I told them what we had done was for their interest, and that it would be a more economic kind of government and a more cooperative situation would prevail. Nobody had any comment to make until an elderly village head said 'That is all very well, sir, I know what you have done, but who now will wipe away our tears?' I was so taken aback by that one and only remark that I was not able to proceed any further with the meeting and I left, but I did feel that it had been a tribute not necessarily to me alone, but to my whole line – that they had wiped tears in their time.

Dividing the spoils

A vast amount of administrative work had to be done before Partition could come into effect. The desk of every official in Calcutta, Delhi and Lahore was piled high with seemingly impossible paperwork. The assets and liabilities of British India had to be divided between India and Pakistan on the basis of 82.5 per cent for India and 17.5 per cent for Pakistan. The army and police, civil service and revenue service, all had to be dismantled and reassembled, as did everything from railways and schools through to trucks, paper, pens and paperclips. In just one month the accumulation of centuries of British hoarding, storing, building and creating was turned up, turned out and meticulously divided between the two soon-to-be dominions. But these were, in essence, things. Yet the division of these 'things' impacted on the lives of millions of people, too often with devastating effect.

Carnage

Millions of Hindus, Muslims and Sikhs were terrified that, after independence, they would wake up on the wrong side of the India–Pakistan border, living in a country hostile to their faith. They abandoned their

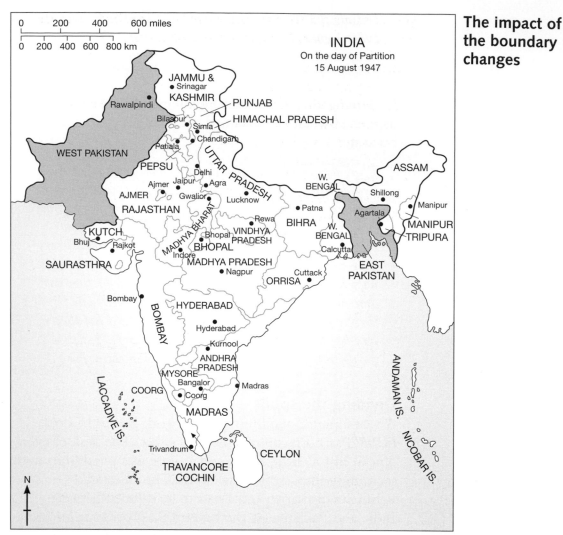

The impact of the boundary changes

INDIA
On the day of Partition
15 August 1947

homes, their fields and their livelihoods; packed what possessions they had, and went. They walked, crammed into bullock carts and tried to make it through to the railway system. They travelled, so they thought, to safety. And as they travelled, Muslims heading west were butchered by Sikhs and Hindus in India. Hindus and Sikhs moving east were murdered by Muslims in Pakistan. It is reckoned that 10 million people tried to change lands in that summer of 1947 and around 1 million Indians never made it to their promised land. They were massacred in an orgy of senseless bloodletting.

Robert Mayne, a British jute merchant travelling near the new border in 1947 found himself helpless:

> *Between Amritsar and Lahore there was mile upon mile of people going east and going west, carrying their belongings. The Hindus and Sikhs from Pakistan moving on one side of the road, the Mohammedans on the other. We stopped and were watching the people go by when a figure came out from the huge line of refugees, stood to attention and asked me to help him. He then said that he'd been with the 4th Indian Division through the desert and in Italy. What could I do to help him? All I could do was look at him and say, ' Your politicians asked for Swaraj, and this is Swaraj.'*

(Quoted in Charles Allen (ed.) *Plain Tales from the Raj*)

Similarly, in 1947 the BBC reporter Wynford Vaughan Thomas was in the Punjab:

> *I used to see these massacres taking place. People tried to cut people down. It was most extraordinary, in the middle of all these scenes, that nobody for a moment touched me or any European. The trains ran a serious risk. Drivers would shunt into a siding and go off to water the engine. That would give the Sikh bands a chance to come in and they would go right through the train and kill everybody. And the train would*

> *shunt on to Lahore where in a siding they would have to take the dead out. They were a terrible sight. You could see them coming with the fly swarms around them. And when the bodies were taken out and laid down, there would be about two thousand at a time. One station official turned to me, he'd obviously been used to order — the pride of British India was the railways — and in a voice I will never forget, he said 'Sir, it is hardly worth issuing tickets any more.' A good man horrified by the collapse of order.*

(Quoted in Charles Allen (ed.) *Plain Tales from the Raj*)

A town in the Punjab after days of Hindu–Muslim rioting

A totally inadequate force of 50,000 troops was dispatched to bring order along the new frontiers. They mostly kept their heads down in their barracks, totally unable to do anything to control the situation. Indeed, Mountbatten himself believed that the British were powerless to prevent the violence of 1946–8:

It is doubtful whether more could have been done had more time been available. British troops were not used. The instructions of the Government were that they were only to be used to protect European lives. No Indian leader would have agreed to use British troops. Military action alone cannot stop large-scale disturbances in the Indian subcontinent. The form of the disturbance and the areas involved make the soldiers' task an impossible one.

Jawaharlal Nehru in 1947 with his daughter Indira and grandson Rajiv. He was to be prime minister of India from 1947 to 1964. Indira and Rajiv also became prime ministers of India.

INDEPENDENCE AT LAST

In Delhi's Constituent Assembly, as midnight on
14 August 1947 approached, Jawaharlal Nehru spoke:

> *Long years ago we made a tryst with destiny, and now the*
> *time comes when we shall redeem our pledge, not wholly or*
> *in full measure, but very substantially. At the stroke of*
> *the midnight hour, when the world sleeps, India will*
> *awake to life and freedom. A moment comes, which comes*
> *but rarely in history, when we step out from the old to the*
> *new, when an age ends, and when the soul of a nation,*
> *long suppressed, finds utterance.*

What of the other main players?

Mountbatten, hoping to be the first Governor General of
both India and Pakistan, had to be content with the
governor generalship of India alone.

Jinnah flew from Delhi to Karachi on 7 August, to
become Pakistan's first Governor General himself.

And Gandhi? He did not want to stay in Delhi for
independence celebrations but left for Bengal. On
Independence Day he wrote:

> *The rot began with the alien government. We, the*
> *inheritors, have not taken the trouble to rectify the errors*
> *of the past.*

SUMMARY QUESTIONS

1 Why, after the Second World War, did Britain need
   to lose its Indian Empire?

2 How far can the failure of the Cabinet Mission be
   blamed on Jawaharlal Nehru?

3 To what extent was Jinnah's call for 'Direct Action' a
   complete mistake?

4 Were the rulers of the princely states treated fairly in
   the months before Partition?

5 Independence was accompanied by appalling violence.
   Who was to blame for this: Jinnah, Nehru or
   Mountbatten?

OVER-ARCHING QUESTIONS

These questions need a knowledge and understanding of the dynamics of Indian history across the whole period 1900–47.

- After the First World War, Hindus and Muslims were prepared to work together. Why, then, after the end of the Second World War was no such rapprochement possible?
- At what point in 1900–47 did the emergence of a separate Pakistan become inevitable?
- To what extent would you agree with the view that Indian independence would have happened without the input of Gandhi?
- How far would you agree with the view expressed by Gandhi that 'The rot began with the alien government. We, the inheritors, have not taken the trouble to rectify the errors of the past'?
- Does the bloodletting and violence that accompanied Partition mean that Gandhi's non-violent methods, as advocated by him in his *satyagraha* campaigns, were useless?

EPILOGUE

Indian independence gave 4 hundred million people freedom from the largest empire the world has ever known. But, as you have seen it was freedom at a price. That price was partition and riot, dislocation and destruction, rape, abduction and death.

The speed with which independence was granted and the way in which it was managed left a number of unresolved issues, but in many ways 1947 was a year of transition rather than one of abrupt closure.

CONTINUITY

- Many British people stayed on in India after 1947 as ordinary civilians and as officials. The governors of the Punjab, Madras, Bombay and the North-West Frontier Province, as well as some service chiefs and 83 civilian officers, stayed in their jobs at least until the early 1950s. Indeed Mountbatten himself, at Nehru's request, stayed on for a year as India's constitutional Governor General.
- For at least 30 years after 1947, the Indian tea industry remained in British hands.
- The Indian Administrative Service took over from the old Indian Civil Service. In the mid-1960s, when there were 23 central secretariat departments, ICS-trained men headed 19 of them.
- The constitutions of both India and Pakistan were framed in accordance with the old 1935 Government of India Act: there are 250 identical clauses.
- The vast number of manuals and handbooks, forms and certificates, maps and gazetteers that were part of the Raj's bureaucracy remained in place for the use of the new administrators.

UNRESOLVED ISSUES

- Partition resulted in an enormous refugee problem as displaced people, once they had located themselves in Hindu India or Muslim Pakistan, had to find somewhere to live and somewhere to work. The refugee problem did not only result in these practical issues. Enormous psychological damage was done to families who were decimated by death or who lost each other in the mass exodus and were never reunited.

- A member of the Hindu Mahasabha, angered at Gandhi's insistence that the Congress government should continue transferring assets to Pakistan, killed him. On 30 January 1948, Naturam Godse shot Gandhi as he addressed a prayer meeting in Delhi.

- The creation of the separate state of Pakistan did not bring unalloyed joy to all Muslims living in the subcontinent. Many of them, particularly those living in the south, simply could not travel to Pakistan. More than 30 million remained behind in India, either through force of circumstance or through choice. Bengali Hindi-speaking Muslims had problems, too, and would mostly have preferred to live in an independent Bengal defined by culture rather than religion; they were alarmed when the Pakistan government announced that Urdu would be the official language of Pakistan.

- Muslims who did make it through to Pakistan tended to be better educated and richer than the local Sindhis and Punjabis and they filled most of the responsible posts in the new government. This caused considerable friction and many *muhajirs*, as they were called, were attacked and had their property looted and burned. One of the first victims was Pakistan's first Prime Minister, Liaquat Ali Khan, who was assassinated in 1951.

- The separation of the state of Pakistan into East and West Pakistan did not make for ease of government and appropriate distribution of resources. In 1971, Pakistan suffered partition again when East Pakistan became the independent state of Bangladesh.

- Conflict arose between Pakistan and India over Kashmir. It was caused largely by the inability of the Hindu maharaja, Hari Singh, to make up his mind as to whether to choose India or Pakistan which resulted in mass killings in 1947–8 and remained unresolved for decades.

In 1947, all the people involved in Partition agreed that power should be transferred on the basis of dominion status; hence both India and Pakistan had a constitutional Governor General. In the case of India, this was Lord

Louis Mountbatten and, in the case of Pakistan, Jinnah. But Britain made it clear that there would be no objection if either state decided, at a later date, to sever all allegiance to the Crown. In 1950, India became a republic, followed, six years later, by Pakistan.

AS ASSESSMENT FOR EDEXCEL

Colonial Rule and the Nationalist Challenge in India c.1900-47 is one of the examination papers set by Edexcel in their Unit 3. The aim of this section is to help you to understand what it is that the examiner will be looking for in your answers and to explain what you have to do to answer the questions successfully.

What are the question targets?

When examiners set questions, they don't just pluck them out of the air! Every question has a specific target, and it's important that you understand what these targets are so that you can focus your answer accordingly.

In Edexcel's Unit 3, you will have to answer one two-part question from a choice of two. In doing this, you will have to show, overall, that you can

- remember, select and organise your historical knowledge so that you answer the question directly
- present historical explanations, showing that you understand what is going on, in a clear and effective way.

However, the (a) and the (b) part of each question have different targets.

(a) is set to test your ability to remember information and to explain the key features of an historical event

(b) is set to test your ability to make and support a judgement about a cause, consequence or key feature.

This means, of course, that you will have to be very clear when you answer the (a) question that you are expected to write an explanation; when you answer the (b) question you must make a judgement and that judgement must be supported by reference to what you know.

What sort of questions will be asked?

The examiner will aim to set questions that remind you of the sort of approach you should take.

(a) These questions will be set and will ask you to explain the causes of an event, or the focus may be on the key features of a development or on the role of an individual. The sort of question stems you should expect are:

- Explain why …
- How do you account for?
- Describe the main stages by which …
- Describe the main features of …
- In what ways did ….?
- What impact did …?

(b) These questions will be set and will ask you to reach a judgement. This judgement may be about the cause or consequence of an historical episode, or it could be about other important key features. In all cases you will need to analyse the situation and reach a judgement that you can support with your own knowledge. The sort of question stems you should expect are:

- How serious was …?
- How significant were …?
- How far did …?
- How successful was …?
- How effective was …?

What are the mark tariffs for each question?

The (a) question will always carry a tariff of 20 marks and the (b) question, a tariff of 40 marks. You will have 55 minutes altogether to answer the (a) and the (b) questions, so it is important that you allocate your time appropriately. It would be sensible to spend about 20 minutes on the (a) question and about 35 minutes on the (b) question. Remember that there is no carry-over of marks from one sub-question to the next, so don't be tempted to spend a long time on the (a) question.

Answering the questions: the Golden Rules

1 **Plan** your answer. This involves working out what information you are going to use and how you will use it either to provide an explanation or to support a judgement.

2 **Support** what you say with carefully selected evidence. The evidence you select must be relevant to the point you are making. Remember you are not trying to impress the examiner with how much you know, but with how you can use what you know to make or support a point.

3 **Think** carefully and try to reach independent conclusions based on the evidence you are presenting. The examiner will not expect you to be original, but will expect you to have reflected on what you have read in this and other books.

4 **Analyse** throughout your answer and not just in a concluding paragraph. Analysis should be evident in the way you plan your answer to present an explanation or a judgement. Remember the difference between narrative (describing what is going on) and analysis (explaining what is happening and presenting your own argument))

5 **Allocate** your time, making sure you don't spend too long on the (a) part of the question

6 **Communicate** your ideas clearly. This involves structuring your answer so that each paragraph makes a separate, supported point, and using correct grammar and spelling.

PRACTICE QUESTIONS

First, here are two (a) questions of the type you are likely to find on the examination paper.

> (a) What impact did the Rowlatt Acts of 1919 have on the British Raj and the Indian people?

Preparation

In order to answer this question, you will need to read the section on the effects of the Rowlatt Acts (pages 63–64 in chapter 3) and about the Amritsar massacre in chapter 4.

What is the question asking you to do?

The question asks you to explain the outcomes of the Rowlatt Acts as they affected both the Raj and Indians.

How to answer the question

- Plan your answer before you start by sorting out the information you will need to use. Here, you will need to:

  - Identify the main features of the Rowlatt Acts
  - Describe the impact these features had on the Raj, with specific examples.
  - Describe the impact these features had on the Indian people, with specific examples.
  - Explain how the Rowlatt Acts led to deterioration in relationships between the Raj and the Indians.

Now carefully look through chapters 3 and 4, finding relevant information that you will need to include and make notes under each of the four headings above.

- Structure your answer. This is a possible structure:
  - Introduction: begin with an opening statement that sets out clearly the direction in which your answer is to go.
  - Development: here you should show your understanding of the main issues and support them by reference to specific examples.
  - Conclusion: this should be brief, to the point, and sum up your explanation.

- Now go ahead and write an answer to the question.

  Remember to support the points you make by direct reference to factual material.

  Remember to write in short paragraphs, making sure each paragraph contains a developed, supported point.

  Remember to check your spelling and grammar

You were given a lot of help in structuring your answer to the (a) question on the impact of the Rowlatt Acts. Now use what you have learned to answer this question:

(a) Explain why Jinnah wanted a separate state for Muslim Indians.

How did you do?

- You should, at the very least, have been able to make simple statements such as:

  The Rowlatt Acts meant that the British could imprison Indians without putting them on trial first.

  Jinnah didn't trust Congress to be fair to Muslims

But this won't get you very far. An answer consisting of simple statements like these will score between 1 and 6 marks out of 20. You want to do better than that!

- You need to give much more detail about the topic. For example, your answer might contain paragraphs like this:

  The Rowlatt Acts of 1919 proposed that the old wartime controls should be brought back. These included imprisonment without trial, censorship and house arrest of suspects. Viceroy Chelmsford pushed the Acts through the Imperial legislative

*Council, even though every Indian member of the Legislative
Council opposed them.*

Or this:

*In 1927, Jinnah offered Congress a deal. He said he would end
the Muslim League's support of separate electorates if Congress
guaranteed Muslims a third of the seats in the central
Legislative assembly. Congress turned him down and this is
where Jinnah's belief that a separate state for Muslims was the
only way forward.*

An answer written in this way will gain you between 7 and 16
marks out of 20.

- If you want to do even better than this, you will have to make
  sure that you draw out the implications of the information you
  are giving when you construct your explanation. For example,
  you might use phrases like these:

*The Rowlatt Acts of 1919 proposed that the old wartime controls
should be brought back. These included imprisonment without
trial, censorship and house arrest of suspects. Viceroy Chelmsford
pushed the Acts through the Imperial legislative Council, even
though every Indian member of the Council opposed them.*

*In this way the Acts suggested that the British had no intention
of relaxing their hold on India. Indeed, they were prepared to
use force to crush Indian opposition. Thus the Rowlatt Acts
alienated a wide range of public opinion in India.*

*In 1927, Jinnah offered Congress a deal. He said he would end
the Muslim League's support of separate electorates if Congress
guaranteed Muslims a third of the seats in the Central
Legislative Assembly and the separation of Sind from Bombay
in order to create a Muslim dominated province. Congress turned
him down. Jinnah tried again in 1929 with a fourteen-point
compromise plan. His offer was again rejected.*

*In these ways Jinnah had hoped to bring Congress and the
Muslim League back together in order to fight together for
India's independence. Referring to the situation as the 'parting of
the ways', from this point Jinnah began to realise that the only
future for Muslim Indians was in a separate state.*

If your answers are structured like this, then you will gain
between 17 and 20 marks.

Now we are going to 'unpack' a (b) question

> (b) 'The British ruled India and did not, in the years 1900-1919, involve the Indian people in any way.' To what extent do you agree with this view of the way in which India was governed in the early years of the twentieth century?

Preparation
You will need to read Chapters 2 and 3 of this book.

What is the question asking you to do?
This style of question is one that is commonly used for a (b) sub-question. You are given a statement and asked to reach a judgement about whether or not you agree with it. You will never be simply asked 'Do you agree with this view?' but will be asked 'How far do you agree with this view', or 'To what extent do you agree with this view?' In other words, you will need to evaluate the amount of agreement you have with the given view by weighing the evidence, both for and against, and reaching a judgement.

Here, you are being asked to reach a judgement about the the level of involvement of the Indian people in the governing of their country.

How to answer the question
- Plan your answer before you start by sorting out the information you will need to use. Here, you will need to:
  - Identify the main features of the way in which India was governed in 1900. This will include those areas that came directly under the Raj and those that were governed indirectly, through the Indian princes.
  - Identify those areas of government in which Indians did participate and the level of that participation
  - Identify those areas of government from which Indians were excluded, either directly, because the rules didn't allow it, or indirectly by making it very difficult for them to do so.
  - Consider the impact of the Morley-Minto reforms of 1909 on the involvement of Indians in government
  - Consider the impact of the Montagu-Chelmsford report and the Government of India Act 1919 on the involvement of Indians in government

Now examine chapters 2 and 3, finding relevant information that you will need to include and make notes under each of the five headings above.

- Structure your answer. This is a possible structure:

  - Introduction: this should set out the case you are going to make.
  - Development: here you should show your understanding of the main issues involved when considering the extent to which Indians did participate in the governing of their own country. You must support what you say and the conclusions you reach by reference to specific examples.
  - Conclusion: this should be brief, to the point, and sum up your line of argument.

- Now go ahead and write an answer to the question.

  Remember to support the points you make by direct reference to factual material.

  Remember to write in short paragraphs, making sure each paragraph contains a developed, supported point.

  Remember to weigh the evidence you have before reaching a conclusion as to the extent to which the 'view' you were given in the question is correct.

  Remember to check your spelling and grammar

You were given a lot of help in structuring your answer to the (b) question on the involvement of Indians in the governing of their country up to 1919. Now use what you have learned to answer this question:

(b) How effective was Gandhi in establishing an independence movement in India between 1919 and 1939?

How did you do?

- You should, at the very least, have been able to make simple statements such as:

  The Indian Councils Act of 1909 said that sixty Indians were to be elected to serve on the viceroy's executive council.

  In 1930 Gandhi decided to oppose the government tax on salt and headed a march of thousands in protest.

But this, as with the (a) question, won't get you very far. An answer consisting of simple statements like these will score between 1 and 8 marks out of 40. You want to do better than that!

- You need to give much more detail about the topic. For example, your answer might contain paragraphs like these:

  The reforms that were proposed by John Morley, the Secretary of State for India, and viceroy Minto were turned into the India Councils Act of 1909. By this Act, sixty Indian representatives were to be elected to the viceroy's executive council, although officials remained in the majority. However, the provincial councils were to be enlarged so that non-officials were in the majority.

  After Gandhi's arrest in 1930, the civil disobedience campaign changed direction. Congress authorised provincial committees to organise their own satyagrahas. Congress said that they should consider focusing on salt, boycotting foreign cloth and refusing to pay taxes.

An answer written in this way will gain you between 9 and 20 marks out of 40.

- If you want to do better than this, you will have to make sure that you use the information and turn it into an explanation. For example, you might use phrases like this:

  By far the most important effect of the Morley-Minto reforms was that, from 1909 onwards, Indian were involved in policy making both in India and, because of john Morley's nominations, in Britain too. Indians were legally entitled to have their views heard.

  In many ways, the decision to oppose the salt tax was a sensible one. The Raj wasn't likely to feel particularly challenged because it brought in very little by way of revenue into the government. But because salt was the one commodity everyone needed, a tax on salt was an emotive issue that united thousands of Indians behind Gandhi in his opposition to the Raj.

An answer written in this way will gain you between 21 and 35 marks out of 40.

In order to hit the top level, and gain between 36 and 40 marks, you will need to have a sustained argument threaded through your whole answer. This will need to support a specific case or point of view, whilst at the same time acknowledging that there is evidence for alternative cases. You must show that you have weighed carefully all the relevant evidence before reaching a judgement, and all the points you make must be fully and accurately supported.

You have now worked through four questions of the type that will appear on the examination paper and you should be able to approach the examination with confidence.

Good luck!

BIBLIOGRAPHY

Many books have been written about the ending of the Raj and Indian independence. Some are general accounts and some deal with specific topics in depth. The following are particularly useful:

BOOKS

Bipan Chandra et al., *India's struggle for Independence 1857–1947,* Penguin (1989)

Judith M. Brown, *Modern India: the Origins of an Asian Democracy*, Oxford University Press (1985)

L. Collins and D. Lapierre, *Freedom at Midnight*, Harper Collins (1997)

Ian Copland, *India 1885–1947*, Longman (2001)

M. N. Das, *India under Morley and Minto*, London (1964)

Alfred Draper, *The Amritsar Massacre*, Buchan & Enright (1985)

P. W .Fay, *The Forgotten Army: India's Armed Struggle for Independence,* University of Michigan (1993)

Patrick French, *Liberty or Death: India's Journey to Independence and Division*, Harper Collins (1998)

Lawrence James, *Raj: the Making and Unmaking of British India*, LBC (1997)

Ayesha Jalal, *Sole Spokesman: Jinnah, the Muslim League and the demand for Pakistan*, Cambridge University Press (1985)

John Keay, *A History of India*, Harper Collins (2000)

D. A. Low (ed.), *Congress and the Raj: Facets of the Indian Struggle 1917–47*, Arnold-Heinemann (1977)

Stanley Wolpert, *A New History of India*, Oxford University Press (2004)

MEMOIRS, DIARIES AND CONTEMPORARY ACCOUNTS

Annie Besant, *India Bond or Free? A World problem*, G. P. Putman's Sons Ltd (1926)

A Campbell-Johnson, *A Mission with Mountbatten*, Bombay (1951)

Penderel Moon (ed.), *Wavell: the Viceroy's Journal*, Oxford University Press (1973)

Jawaharlal Nehru, *An Autobiography*, Allied Publishers, Bombay (1962; first published 1936)

Michael O'Dwyer, *India as I Knew it 1885–1925*, Constable (1925)

COLLECTIONS OF DOCUMENTS
Government of Bombay, *Sources for a History of the Freedom Movement in India*, Govt Central Press Bombay (1958)

P N Chopra, *Quit India Movement: British Secret Documents*, Interprint, New Delhi (1986)

Mushirul Hasan (ed.), *India Partitioned: the Other Face of Freedom*, Roli Books, New Delhi (1995)

Raghavan Iyer (ed.), *The Essential Writings of Mahatma Gandhi*, Oxford University Press, Delhi (1996)

N. Mansergh and E. W. R. Lumby, *The Transfer of Power 1942–7*, HMSO (1970)

FICTION
E. M. Forster, *Passage to India*

R. K. Narayan, *Waiting for the Mahatma*

Arundati Roy, *The God of Small Things*

Salman Rushdie, *Midnight's Children*

Paul Scott, *The Raj Quartet*

Paul Scott, *Staying On*

Vikram Seth, *A Suitable Boy*

GLOSSARY

ashram Religious retreat; a religious community around a guru

bagh Garden

babu A clerk; used by the British to describe western educated Indians

Brahmin Hindus belonging to the highest, original priestly, caste

durbar Ruler's open court for his subjects

guru Teacher; religious mentor

hartal Stoppage of work

hajj Pilgrimage to Mecca made by Muslims. One of the five obligations of the Muslim faith

Jat Peasant farming caste

jihad Muslim holy war

khaddar Cotton cloth produced in India

karma The sum of a person's actions which determine the state into which they will be reincarnated

Kshatriya Warrior caste in Hindu society

Maharajha Ruler, king

Mahasabha A Hindu political party

Mahatma Honorofic title meaning 'great soul'

Maratha A member of the princely and military classes of the kingdom of Maharashtra

nabob Englishman returned to Britain with a fortune made in India

nawab Muslim title; a Muslim nobleman

presidency Formal term applied to Bengal, Bombay and Madras, the oldest of the provinces in British India. Originally the senior official in each place was called 'president'

Qur'an (Koran) Islamic scripture as revealed to Muhammad

Raj Rule, particularly British rule in India

Raja Ruler, king

salaam A subservient greeting accompanied with a low bow

salat Performing ritual prayers in the proper way five times a day. One of the five obligations of the Muslim faith

satyagraha Literally 'truth force'; a word invented by Gandhi to refer to non-violent campaigns

sawm Fasting during the month of Ramadan. One of the five obligations of the Muslim faith

sepoy A soldier in the Indian army

shahadah Sincerely reciting the Muslim profession of faith. One of the five obligations of the Muslim faith

shruti Hindu books of authority

Shudra Labouring caste

Smriti Hindu scripture of lesser authority to the main shruti. They contain historical and mythological stories and law books

swaraj Self-rule

Vaishya Trading caste

zakat Giving alms to the poor and needy. One of the five obligations of the Muslim faith

INDEX

References to illustrations are in italic.
References to glossary entries are in bold.
References to key information text are indicated by the suffix *k*.

HEINEMANN ADVANCED HISTORY